Jean-Pierre Cuoni, a Banker with Heart

Christophe Vuilleumier

in collaboration with **Noëlle Demole**

Jean-Pierre Cuoni, a Banker with Heart

Éditions Slatkine
GENÈVE
2022

Transpose SA, www.transpose-ai.com,
was responsible for the translation of this book.
Thank you to all their team for this collaboration.

© 2022. Noëlle Demole.
© 2022. Éditions Slatkine, Genève.
www.slatkine.com
Any reproduction or translation, total or partial, is forbidden
All rights reserved for all countries
ISBN 978-2-8321-1133-8

Acknowledgments

I would especially like to thank from the bottom of my heart Christophe Vuilleumier, Lonnie Howell, Caroline Demole, Claire-Anne Demole, Marie Demole, Yvonne Cuoni, Guenther Greiner, Jean-Pierre Roth, Yves Oltramare and Ivan Slatkine. Without their crucial help over the past two years, this book could not have been written.

Noëlle Demole

Summary

Foreword
    Jean-Pierre Roth 11
    Yves Oltramare 15

Preface 19

Prologue 21

At the beginning 25
    A "Citibanker" 43
    A wedding for life 45
    Private Banking 60

A new era 75
    EFG Private Bank 80
    Entering the stock exchange 101
    A Philanthropic Ideal 111

An active Retirement 117
    EFG in 2022 120
    Jean-Pierre Cuoni's "five ladies" 124
    Shere Khan Youth Protection 134

Epilogue 139

Annexes 144

Our Story 146

Bibliography 151

Notes 155

The authors 159

Foreword

Dear Jean-Pierre,

Fate brought us together!

After all, we must have both been named Jean-Pierre for a reason! Who knows? Maybe both our parents – yours in old Lucerne, mine in just-as-old Valais – thought that being named after two patron saints was better than one. Maybe they were the ones watching over us, putting us on the right path: you into private banking, me into public service at the National Bank.

Actually, we both came from similar backgrounds. You were from a family well-rooted in its local community, always keeping an eye on wider horizons. Not born to wealth, you were from a modest background where hard work was the key to making sure future generations had a better life. Your parents would have liked to know my parents; my mother trained as a teacher and my father worked at the post office. I can easily imagine the talks they would have had about the need to be strict with their children in order to give them a taste for studies and hard work – the only way to ensure future success.

Still, there is one major difference between our two life paths. You were born before the war, while I was born after it. This difference could explain why your mind was more critical and always sharp, while I was always entirely convinced that our country would always be able to weather whatever storm came our way.

And you also "played with banknotes"! In the same way, my father, back when he was in charge of the post office in the village of Saxon, would give me the task of "doing the safe" – that is, counting the office's cashbox before closing for the day. I was fascinated by the stacked-up bundles, all stapled with care. Your career as a future banker was already laid out, just like mine at the central bank.

Both of us were made for economic studies in our own way: you at the Lucerne School of Commerce, me at the economic prep school at the Abbaye de Saint-Maurice. No Greek, Latin or philosophy for us; just accounting, law and the study of economic practices. Everything we learned was concrete. To this day, that has marked our characters, and it was ultimately what allowed us to meet and become friends.

Our pathways were about to go on very separate tracks, but there was one important step left to take: military training. It was unavoidable for our families. Your father was an officer, just like mine. He instilled in you a sense of duty towards your community. It would be unthinkable to have a successful professional life without a military career behind it. You chose the infantry, while I chose artillery. We started as soldiers, then became non-commissioned officers, then finally were made officers, both of us earning the rank of captain. The army taught us not only the meaning of commitment, but also how to push our own limits.

Our paths, which had been parallel for so long, split here, seemingly forever – largely because of your urge to explore the great unknown. You left for Paris, then the United States, starting off on what would become your career in international banking. As for me, I stayed firmly on the path of civil service, obtaining my doctorate degree in cash economics. You studied the mechanisms of finance, while I learned the inner workings of the Swiss economy.

Although our paths were now far apart from each other, I'm sure both of us were looking at the same realities in the financial world. A lot happened in the currency world in the 70s, with the abandonment of the gold standard and the collapse of the Bretton-Woods fixed rates. These were challenges for you as a banker, looking out for your bank and your clients. It was a moment of introspection for me, a future banker at the central bank, worried about the future of the Swiss economy. Those were turbulent times, but we sure learned a lot! We both came out of it stronger: you as a private banker, me with a mastery of the macro-economic world.

Our paths had to meet again! In the early 80s, you were named Vice-Chairman of the Association of Foreign Banks in Switzerland (AFBS); I had just been made a deputy member of general management for the SNB. According to tradition, a delegation from the AFBS must meet with one from the SNB twice a year to share views. We both took part! I can still see you next to Ernest Schaad, the Association Chairman: he was a good deal rounder than you, with all your sharp angles. The viewpoint meetings were always very lively. The Association began to wonder about the future course of interest and exchange rates, while the SNB shared its estimation of the general situation. Still, we never revealed our true intentions, hiding behind safe catchphrases.

This is where our paths began to cross. Our ties grew tighter and friendlier, even outside of our informal meetings. How many times did we run into each other on the train in the early morning? You coming in a bit haggard from French-speaking Switzerland on Monday mornings, me boarding at Bern to get to my Zurich office. It was during those special moments that I discovered your cheerfulness, your smile and your ever-quick wit. We both learned more and more about each other, feeling that we shared the same background and were passionate about the same things.

Our friendship grew stronger over time. Your career took off, going from Citibank, Natwest, Coutts... As for me, I climbed the ranks at the SNB. In 1995, you made your dreams a reality. EFG was the project you had always wanted, something you always spoke of passionately. This was a unique private banking model that allowed you to put into practice all the experience you had built over 30 years. In an extraordinary coincidence, you decided to set up your bank at the end of the Bahnhofstrasse in Zurich, only a stone's throw from the SNB. I could never resist sneaking a peek inside your offices every day on my way to work. There was always a beautiful piece of modern art to admire. That's the sign of a boss aiming for the top!

With you at the head of EFG, and me as Chairman of the SNB, we would often meet at the Club du Baur au Lac. You would tell me about your worries and your experiences; not knowing much in your line of work, I would listen and learn a lot. I remember how original those conversations felt. It was a kind of creativity that I had never felt during meetings with other branch representatives. It's just that you always thought "out of the box" – you weren't from the traditional banking circles in Geneva, Zurich or Basel, but from your Lucerne homeland, sprinkled in with a bit of Anglo-Saxon culture. It was a solid background that gave you a unique outlook on things.

After retirement, our ties became more and more friendly, spreading out to your dear Yvonne and to Floriane, my wife. We left behind Lake Zurich for the beautiful shores of Lake Geneva, in Founex. We spent beautiful nights in excellent company, the meals delicious and perfectly planned. I can still hear your thunderous laugh after a good joke. I can still see your eyes widening in front of the beautiful works of art you chose so carefully, and that you commented on so passionately. And then there was the Buchet I dreamed about so often above your fireplace...

Dear Jean-Pierre, you left us too soon and so abruptly. But your warm, vibrant personality lives on in our hearts.

Jean-Pierre Roth

Before it was a name, Cuoni was a symbol for me – a symbol represented by a group of three arrows, all so solidly bound at the base that nothing could separate them, let alone break them, not even Heaven!

Cuoni: Three arrows and a link, named Yvonne, Jean-Pierre and Caroline

Cuoni, a trio:

> Yvonne, the inspiration
> Jean-Pierre, the doer
> Caroline, the link

Cuoni is above all the extraordinary mystery brought about when two young girls, Caroline and Arielle, met each other over 40 years ago.

Thanks to this unbreakable bond between our two daughters, through some sort of mysterious force, my wife Inez and I were able to forge a lasting friendship with Yvonne and Jean-Pierre.

Memories grow dim as the years go by, so I would like to mention the impression Jean-Pierre's character left behind instead.

Although our friendship started through our daughters, it was able to develop in the professional world.

Although twelve years older than him, what probably most drew me to him when we first met was our shared fascination with New York.

I had started my American career there in the 50s, back when the "sky was the limit" during the post-war years.

We both learned everything from our first employers: Lehman Brothers for me, National City Bank for Jean-Pierre ten years later. It was more than just the dynamism of Wall Street. We felt overcome by the vitality of American culture, the warmth with which we were welcomed, the passion for innovation, the openness that felt like a breath of fresh air while Europe was licking its wounds from WWII and reflecting on its future. We certainly were too idealistic, but that helped us better realise just how much European banks had fallen behind the United States in terms of modern wealth management techniques and "marketing", which was considered a barbaric term at the time. Americanisation was going to impact the entire world; in the 60s, it would inspire Jean-Jacques Servan-Schreiber's "The American Challenge". With 10 million copies published in over 15 languages, it excited both Jean-Pierre and me, as it matched up with what we felt: there was a gap between the North American superpower and the rest of the world.

At age 25, Jean-Pierre was sent to Geneva to prepare for Citibank's expansion into Europe. Relying on our backgrounds, we were sure to bring added value to our new positions.

My aim here is not to illustrate Jean-Pierre Cuoni's brilliant and fascinating career; his granddaughter Noëlle will already do that in this lovely biography. I would just like to finish this short introduction by talking about the man that I met in the field when Jean-Pierre joined me in 1985 on the ILO Pension Fund, where we worked together for several years.

His presentations on the economic and stock situation were always very perceptive, revealing an opinion that was always willing to stir up conversation and break out of the mould. While some responded to periods of uncertainty with timid solutions, Jean-Pierre's positive nature shined through with his optimistic outlook on how the world would evolve long term.

However, Jean-Pierre's real talents were for wealth management. This work brought together his great warmth and his interest in meeting new people around the world, people who were – as he said it himself – "intelligent and cultivated". His affectionate attachment to his clients, combined with his widely-renowned professional skills, made Jean-Pierre a formidable figure in his field.

That can be seen by the clients who followed him whenever he changed establishments. "The client belongs to the manager and not the bank", he liked to repeat. He would also add: "That is a considerable, almost philosophical difference that my competitors refuse to admit".

Jean-Pierre was not sentimental when it came to business; that's something he learned in America!

Jean-Pierre's life was dedicated to a happy, warm household and his professional calling. He was a fighter with a bright smile.

Yves Oltramare

Preface

I have brought this book to life in memory of my grandfather, my "Papou", Jean-Pierre Cuoni, whom I loved dearly. His life, both personal and professional, deserves to be told. It is a life that, I hope, will become ensconced in archives beyond our family ones.

My grandfather's life was filled with positivity and ambition, and he lived it exactly the way he wanted to. "Look, life is so beautiful", he often told me. There's no denying he built himself an extraordinary life.

He always wore the same glasses that would fall off his nose, with a bald head and the same big eyebrows I have, his eyes as blue as the sky. Papou walked like a leader and always had a small smile at the corner of his mouth; he loved people more than anything else. My grandfather was my role model, someone to comfort and support me. His secret was the key to happiness: to like what you have and to always have an unquenchable thirst for life. Both humble and brilliant, he was an extraordinary role model for me and my sisters! His stories, told during a trip or at a wake, have marked me forever, so deeply that even as a child I felt that his life would have to be written down so that not even a snippet would be lost over the years.

My grandfather left us far too soon, but at least he knew how to take advantage of every day that he dedicated to his work or to his family. Papou's legacy is, I believe, the life that he led so brilliantly in so many different areas. Of course, he knew his fair share of obstacles and disappointments, as we all do. Still, he managed to only remember the good and forget the rest, without straying from his own sense of humour. I am convinced that his rare force of character helped him overcome the barriers in his path and make his dreams a reality.

My Papou was an extraordinary, unique person who inspired many of those around him throughout his life. That is why I wanted to put his story to paper, so that it can stand as an example and so that those who come after us will remember him. For his close family, his memory is still alive and felt all around us. How could it be otherwise? My grandfather was such a pillar, a daily light we could turn to for comfort. In spite of his abrupt passing in 2017, my grandfather continues to shape and inspire me through his choices, the projects he brought about and the moral strength that he demonstrated throughout his life.

The text that follows about his life and about the incredible founding of his bank, EFG, is therefore more than just a book to me, but rather an homage I would like to make in his honour. I hope that reading this biography will give you as much pleasure as it has to me.

> After all these adventures in "FlyPapou", I wish you, my Papou, a last great trip as exhilarating as your life has been. I love you.

Noëlle Demole

Prologue

Retracing the steps of a man's life necessarily means stepping into his private thoughts and learning about his hopes and disappointments. It also means evaluating the strength of his character and the world he inhabited throughout his life. All the same, as I'm sure all biographers will agree, depicting someone's life is always a gamble; after all, every individual, whoever they may be, keeps his or her own secrets, a part of themselves in the shadows, a mystery that is better left unexplored. It isn't so much that this mystery helps build a mythos around the person (although that is one of the main ingredients). Rather, breaking down a life with almost scientific precision can be piercingly blunt while their memory still lives on in the hearts of their loved ones. Any historian or commentator who claims to have captured all the aspects of a life shaped by the periods it traversed, a life just as complex and layered as any other, risks a great deal of hubris.

Jean-Pierre Cuoni was a banker!

Though some sneer at his profession today, for him it was more than a career. Jean-Pierre's work was like a profession of faith for decades. It was an ideal, a passion that inspired him from his early childhood, a passion that allowed him to reach the same heights as those who had come before him. He was able to achieve all of his ambitions without ever betraying himself. Jean-Pierre did not come from money. He was not part of a long dynasty of bankers. He started his career humbly, working behind a counter. But he was tenacious – he always said that life was work, and that he would rest once he turned 80. That work ethic, along with his innate business sense and his generosity, helped him found a bank in just 40 years, a bank that would quickly become a real empire.

Jean-Pierre Cuoni had a heart of gold!

He had a unique and brilliant journey, in the same vein as Giovanni de' Medici or Jacob Fugger – or, for a more modern reference, Mayer Rothschild or Amadeo Giannini[1]. As everyone points out, Jean-Pierre was luminous, charismatic and a force for good that anyone could turn to in times of need. His goodwill shines from any archive consulted or any story recounted. Still, he was aware of this side of himself, at least enough to not let himself be taken advantage of by any con artists. Instead, he decided to invest his characteristic openness into the many businesses he dedicated himself to throughout his career, as well as in his friends and family – always demonstrating a great sense of loyalty. Loyalty was more than just a word for him; it was one of his core virtues, something he was able to prove on several occasions. Just look to the forewords to this book for proof of that!

The following pages are dedicated to him.

I would like to thank his friends, EFG of course and, above all else, his family, especially his granddaughter Noëlle, who were able to trust this project and provide me with their family papers and memories. May this book be the imperfect expression of so many beautiful memories of an exceptional man.

[Demole Archives]

PROLOGUE

Erwin Cuoni and his wife Emma [Demole Archives]

At the beginning

"Life is how you look at it."
Jean-Pierre Cuoni

1937! The Spanish Civil War is raging. Guernica has been destroyed in a bombing, inspiring Picasso. At the same time, the Hindenburg disaster is sweeping through the worldwide media. In 1937, the sound of jackboots is thundering across Europe. In the USSR, Stalin has instilled his reign of terror.

And on 8 August of that year in Lucerne, Jean-Pierre Cuoni was born. He was the son of Emma Fuchs, a seamstress working in a woman's fashion workshop, and Erwin Cuoni, a high school teacher who had graduated from the University of Neuchâtel[2]. Erwin acquired Lucerne citizenship for himself and his family in 1943. This allowed him to be named as a Director of Human Resources in the city of Lucerne two years later, as well as being appointed to the Grand Council in 1947 for the *Liberal Party*, a position he would hold until 1963[3]. This was setting down solid roots in Lucerne for a man from Bern and Dittingen! His father, Paul Josef Ermin Cuoni (1872-1960), had come there at the turn of the century. In 1909, he founded a short-lasting company producing levelling and smoothing products, E. Cuoni & Cie[4].

Erwin was a traditional man of habit. He would decide to not correct the error the civil registrar had committed when his father had first inscribed their family name. Instead, he preferred to keep the last name Cuoni, which everyone knew him by, rather than the original name of Cueni. His good nature and his leadership skills soon put themselves to work. He quickly became Chairman of the Bourgeoisie as well as the *Maskenliebhaber Gesselschaft*. Founded in 1819, the latter was a traditional association that managed Lucerne's famous Carnival.

Erwin loved music, and would occasionally take the time to write down certain aspects of local history[5]. He also taught his son about the horrors of war. As a child, Jean-Pierre played football with Hans Erni and may even have crossed paths with a few American soldiers on leave coming to Switzerland from Germany in 1945.

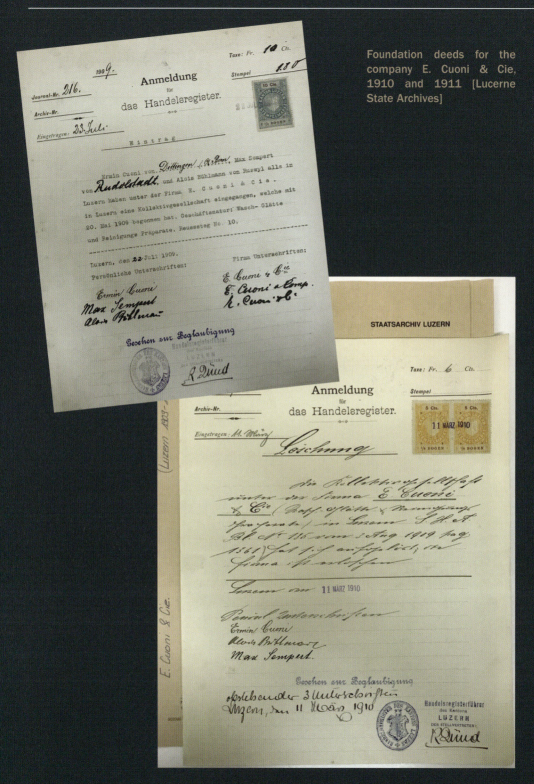

Foundation deeds for the company E. Cuoni & Cie, 1910 and 1911 [Lucerne State Archives]

American soldiers on leave in Lucerne in 1945 [ACL: FDC 76/1866.1]

At age 8, however, this world would slip away from him, as he came occasionally into contact with the Chairman of the Lucerne Cantonal Bank, Hans Pfyffer von Altishofen[6]. A friend of his father's from the same political party, von Altishofen was also a deputy to the Grand Council, a former commander of the Swiss Guard[7] and a colonel in the Swiss army – a higher rank than Erwin's, who was then just a simple adjudant.

Impressed, Jean-Pierre would listen to this gentleman in a felt hat, wing collars and a moustache tell stories of his life: his stint as Swiss Ambassador in Warsaw from 1921 to 1923, or the ways the Swiss

Jean-Pierre Cuoni as a child [Demole Archives]

National Bank had changed since he had become a member of the Council in 1927.

With widened eyes, Jean-Pierre Cuoni was discovering a huge, exotic world, full of possibilities and opportunities for those who knew how to seize them. What was more, the man painting this no doubt very expressive picture for him also had influence over his father!

Jean-Pierre still needed time to grow and learn more about life. However, for the time being he had whole-heartedly swallowed the magic of those words and the power of something that seemed just out of reach: money. The hours he spent not only collecting stamps but also playing "with banknotes" behind an artisanal counter began to sink in, slowly shaping his dreams. In his mind, he already knew what he wanted: he would become a banker!

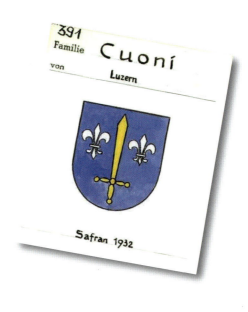

Hans Pfyffer von Altishofen [Dodis.ch/P5631]

Jean-Pierre was the youngest child. Erwin and Emma already had three daughters: Erminia, Ursule and Sonia. The birth of a son felt like a gift from heaven. His mother and sisters adored him, and would often sacrifice a part of their wartime rations to him. Jean-Pierre quickly developed his self-confidence as well as a deep sense of family. "My mother was the one who gave me my strength throughout my life", he would later tell his own family.

Brought up in a liberal family (his father would even have a family crest designed in 1932), Jean-Pierre was a poor student, much to the chagrin of his teachers, who constantly repeated to his parents that he would never be successful in his studies. Stubborn, his mother would always reply that all that meant was that his teachers didn't understand anything about her son, and that he was of course the best student. Although Emma Cuoni couldn't of course see the future, she knew about her child's potential. The future would prove her right!

Erminia, Ursule, Sonia and Jean-Pierre at Christmas 1940 [Demole Archives]

Jean-Pierre as a child [Demole Archives]

AT THE BEGINNING

Jean-Pierre witnessing with his father General Guisan's visit to Sempach in 1945 [Demole Archives]

For the time being, however, Jean-Pierre spent a peaceful life in Lucerne, enjoying a happy childhood in a loving family. In the spring of 1952, he attended the International Exposition of Photography, drawing hundreds of artists from around the world to the shadows of the *Kapellbrücke*. Three years later, at age 18, he would listen to his father speak enthusiastically about the 7th Congress of the World Liberal Union that would take place in Lucerne. At that time, Erwin's political party was moving full steam ahead, bringing about a wave of liberalism in Lucerne. That same year, the liberals celebrated the inauguration of the first highway built in Switzerland, linking Lucerne with Ennethorw. In 1956, Jean-Pierre attended yet another new project from his father's party: the inauguration of the cable car that brought tourists to the summit of Mount Pilatus.

Inauguration of the Pilatus cable car in 1956[8]

Class of 1955 [Demole Archives]

This wiped out any doubts that the dragons from the medieval legends could still be lurking in the mountain. Instead, it was a time for modernity and progress! Jean-Pierre's eyes were focused on the future, especially at a time where any project seemed possible for those who could dream. He quickly obtained a degree in banking and commerce at the Lucerne School of Commerce.

Jean-Pierre Cuoni as a young man [Demole Archives]

1955. James Dean was dominating movie posters with *A Rebel Without a Cause*, and all Jean-Pierre could think about was getting to the United States. A new graduate at 18 years old, the young man dreamed of heading to America, the country where anything was possible.

> "At the time, Switzerland offered 500 visas per year for its citizens to move to America. But to get a visa, you needed to get a job. And to get a job, you needed a visa."
>
> Jean-Pierre Cuoni

Thinking that working for an American company would help him get a visa more quickly, it didn't take long for him to find a job at the American Express Bank. It was a first, two-year experience that, although it took place in Switzerland, sparked his personal "Americanisation" and greatly improved his English.

Jean-Pierre Cuoni as a young man [Demole Archives]

At 20 years old, Jean-Pierre was forced to submit to Swiss law and put on a uniform to fulfil his military service. He became an infantry captain. However, his American dream had not died.

Recruit Jean-Pierre Cuoni in 1957 [Demole Archives]

Corporal Jean-Pierre Cuoni in 1959 [Demole Archives]

Captain Jean-Pierre Cuoni in 1960 [Demole Archives]

Goodbye American Express Bank, hello Citibank!

Having done his service, Jean-Pierre continued to pursue his dream by finding a position with Citibank in Paris, on the Champs-Elysées. It was another American bank that could potentially help him finally cross the Atlantic.

Founded in 1812 in New York, Citibank had been operating in Paris since 1906; for the young Swiss man, this new professional experience was an extraordinary opportunity. Not only had he managed to work within a prestigious international institution, but he also had the chance to learn French.

Jean-Pierre Cuoni during the 1950s [Demole Archives]

Although the newspapers kept relating the bloody events taking place in Algeria, Jean-Pierre decided to leave Lucerne for France. In any case, there were no safety concerns about heading to Paris in 1957, as the war raging in North Africa, as well as the attacks from freedom fighters, had yet to reach the capital. He left home with 300 francs in his pocket and a bag with a few clothes. Only his father had any qualms about the strength of his character. Sitting down in the family living room at Landschaustrasse 19, poring over a newspaper, he told his son without lifting his eyes: *"You won't make it. I know you'll be back home in a few days"*[9]. He was doubtful, but also likely disappointed. Erwin had hoped for a long time that Jean-Pierre would study law. That would not happen.

And so Jean-Pierre left his childhood home at age 23. In 1957 it was a small city, a city where most people knew each other but one that was still open to the world thanks to the many tourists that came to admire the medieval wooden bridges. In doing so, he left behind him the comfortable Wesemlin house where he and his sisters had passed countless summers playing in the garden. What did he feel when he reached the City of Lights? When he saw the Seine, Notre Dame and Saint-Germain-des-Prés for the first time? Almost certainly a bit of pride, and an amused thought about his father's scepticism.

"At the time, working in a Swiss bank seemed like the greatest profession in the world."

Jean-Pierre Cuoni

JEAN-PIERRE CUONI, A BANKER WITH HEART

Of course, back then, he had no idea he would work for Citibank for 28 years – especially seeing as the beginning wasn't easy. Huddled in a precarious maid's room that leaked in the rain, his pay was so poor he couldn't buy a newspaper every morning; he even had to put his entire salary into a meal for his first date. Still, this did not dampen Jean-Pierre's ambition. "One day I'm going to be the chairman of a bank", he said to the young woman he had invited, who had been amazed by his gusto.

Jean-Pierre was in Paris, a city filled with energy. From a walk in the Jardins du Luxembourg, you could feel the hum of the words of Sartre and Gréco, dream along to the clarinet while thinking of Boris Vian or Jano Merry during jam sessions in the city's jazz clubs. They were carefree years where hard work and talent were rewarded. What did he have to be afraid of when there was everything to win? All he needed was to prove his worth. He was a bank teller at Citibank, greeting clients, counting francs and dollars and keeping the register. He would change currency on Monday, cash in amortisations on Tuesday and deliver register receipts on Wednesday. He quickly became the symbol of Swiss precision, guaranteeing the gravitas of the institution.

Jean-Pierre Cuoni as a jazz player
[Demole Archives]

The Parisian years of Jean-Pierre [Demole Archives]

But Jean-Pierre had more than just his precision. He also had an important advantage: the ability to speak English with English-speaking clients.

His colleagues would praise him for his qualities: his discipline, his team spirit, his loyalty, his politeness and his respect. Jean-Pierre would make this his credo. During a moment of reflection, he would even write down his "Life Plan" focusing on these values, although he would also add love[10]! Starting out as a simple teller, he quickly rose through the ranks. In a short time, his higher-ups signed him up for an executive traineeship programme for three years.

> "I saw these 50 year old senior managers in striped suits and buttoned-down shirts and I thought, I want to be one of them one day, I want to be the chairman of the bank."
>
> Jean-Pierre Cuoni

A "Citibanker"

Jean-Pierre Cuoni would become a Citibanker. The company he had started working for had a long history, full of surprises, and its background inevitably marked those that came into contact with it. First the City Bank of New York, then the First National City Bank of New York, it had been for a long time one of the most important banks in the United States. One of the most important, but also one of the oldest. It was founded by Samuel Osgood, a revolutionary who had made a name for himself at the end of the American War of Independence in the late 18th century. Citibank had played a non-negligible role in financing the War of 1812, a war the Americans had fought against the British. It also supported the Union in 1861 during the American Civil War and helped finance the Panama Canal in 1904.

Jean-Pierre in Paris in 1961
[Demole Archives]

Although in 1929 it had been accused of spearheading a policy that led to the Wall Street crash, the bank had rebuilt its reputation by managing 5.6 billion dollars for the US Treasury during the Second World War, thus taking part in the Allied war effort and helping defeat the Axis forces. Chaired by James Stillman Rockefeller from 1952 to 1967, Citibank put the first credit cards on the market with the "Everything Card" in 1967. It would then join forces with Mastercard, reorganising into a holding that year under the name of Citicorp, although the name Citibank still prevails in the public mind. Established in nineteen countries with over 2,600 branches around the world, the company that Jean-Pierre would play a key role in was an empire.

In 1963, Jean-Pierre already had several years of experience with Citibank. He had completed the executive traineeship with ease, and once his employer decided to open an office in Geneva at Rue du Rhône, offered him, being Swiss himself, the chance to join the team when the doors to the new bank opened.

Citibank today, Geneva [Public domain]

A wedding for life

His new assignment radically changed the course of his life. One night, having stayed late at the office, he saw a woman in the middle of a hallway. The sight made him freeze in his tracks. The beautiful stranger had just come to visit her sister, who worked in the institution. From that moment on, the memory of her stuck with him to the point that he asked his employee about the woman that had become his muse. His intern, who would later become his sister-in-law, told him not to bother. Yvonne, the stranger in the night, was already engaged at the time.

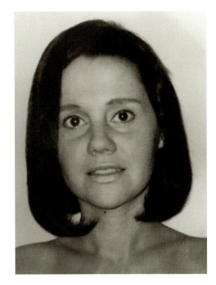

Yvonne Haltiner [Demole Archives]

With breathtaking gusto, Jean-Pierre apparently told her that "engaged wasn't married". These words would become a sort of motto for the young man during the years that followed.

However, at the time, Jean-Pierre had only started his conquest. He would have to wait for a rainy night to start to stand a chance. That night, the young woman and her sister, having spent the afternoon at the Lake Geneva beaches, were stuck in torrential rain.

Publicity 1966 [CIG]

Jean-Pierre and Yvonne [Demole Archives]

Just to tease her, Yvonne asked her sister, *"Why don't you call that young man at the bank and get him to help us? Since he's always asking about me and flirting with me."* A knight in shining armor, Jean-Pierre came running. From that point on, he showered her with flowers just as much as she filled his dreams.

She finally gave into his advances. Inviting him out with her sister for honour's sake, she interrupted their drinks by asking abruptly, *"So, it seems you want to get to know me?"* She then explained a bit mockingly that she was engaged. That was when Jean-Pierre answered, *"But I don't want to be engaged to you – I want to marry you!"* With a bit of machismo, he promised her the moon, and said he would take her around the world. She quickly fell under his spell. They were married in his hometown of Lucerne.

> **"You take care of me, I take care of you."**
>
> **Jean-Pierre Cuoni**

AT THE BEGINNING

Wedding of Yvonne Haltiner and Jean-Pierre Cuoni, 24 April 1965 [Demole Archives]

> "The difference is when you love someone."
>
> **Jean-Pierre Cuoni**

In 1966, Citibank opened a second office in Zurich. Once again, Jean-Pierre took part in opening this establishment. For the occasion, he bought "American Flag", one of the major works by key American Pop artist Jasper Johns. It would be enthroned in the lobby for years after. This delighted Jean-Pierre. His passion for art and paintings led him, even at that moment, to build a collection of works including pieces by Hodler and pop art artists such as Jasper Johns, on the fringe of his fad for Swiss currency!

He oversaw the opening of the new bank for only a year, as in 1967 a new challenge awaited him. In fact, the bank's leadership had asked him to come work in New York. His dream had been achieved. He left for the United States. 1967 was a big year! Not only did he achieve a professional dream, but what's more, he also became a father. On 24 July, his daughter Caroline was born, filling him with joy.

Jean-Pierre Cuoni and his daughter Caroline, 1969
[Demole Archives]

Previous page: Yvonne Cuoni and her daughter Caroline [Demole Archives]

JEAN-PIERRE CUONI, A BANKER WITH HEART

In May of that year, the international community adopted the Kennedy Round, which let the fifty nations making up 80% of worldwide trade reduce customs tariffs by 40%. This quickly inflated financial flow across the planet, even as the Six-Day War flared up in Israel and the surrounding Arab countries, as Che Guevara was shot down in October and as American pacifist movements protested in Washington against the Vietnam War. The world was churning, and Jean-Pierre had finally arrived on American soil.

He witnessed the social revolution that started in Paris in 1968 from afar; it wasn't long before the effects began to be seen in the United States, encouraging waves of protest from students at Columbia University, opposed to not only the war but also segregation and conservatism in general. Jean-Pierre was 31 at the time. As a foreigner in a country where anything was possible, his world revolved around numbers, projects and long hours of hard work. Earning the trust and respect of his colleagues, his responsibilities grew very quickly.

> "Americans are great. They give responsibility very quickly to young people, and I benefitted from that."
>
> Jean-Pierre Cuoni

He ended up spending three years in New York, buzzing with the rhythm of Wall Street but also the big events of the time. So far away from calm, like-minded little Switzerland! In April 1968, the assassination of Martin Luther King in Memphis left him stunned. How could the United States hold two such different realities? The same "land of the free" that had sent men to the moon in July 1969 was the place where King had been killed the year before – the same year as Robert Francis Kennedy, the brother of President Kennedy who had been killed in 1963.

The American experience, teeming with ambiguities, successes, hard work and opportunities, had to have made Jean-Pierre realise that some limits were made to be shattered, while some values needed to be defended! Jean-Pierre would continue to push against these limits. Along with his daily work for the bank in New York, every evening he attended a continuing education programme in finance set up by Harvard University. Afterwards, when he wasn't too tired, Jean-Pierre and his wife would drive around Manhattan. At those moments, the couple felt like "the kings of the world".

Jean-Pierre Cuoni returned to Switzerland in 1970, bolstered by an intense experience, a sizeable network that gave him international connections and an idea that, once he had it, he couldn't let go of.

> "I came back from New York, and I had this great idea of creating a worldwide private banking model for Citibank."
>
> Jean-Pierre Cuoni

Citibank was spreading more and more around the world; in 1969 alone, it associated itself with the Banque internationale pour l'Afrique Occidentale, with the National and Grindlays Bank in London and the Iranian Bank in Tehran within the realm of French economic influence[11]. At the same time, ever since his return to Switzerland, Jean-Pierre was working on a business banking model based on American models, while completing his training at the prestigious IMD business school in Lausanne.

The Geneva office had moved in 1970 to a modern building on Place du Lac. Jean-Pierre's goal was to concentrate part of Citibank's Swiss branch's activities on securities trading and asset management without calling on the public for funds on deposit. This way, the bank would not have to maintain the ratio of equity capital to total liabilities as required by law, and would not have to publish annual accounts and an interim balance sheet.

The time was right. Even if the United States was under fire from protests against the war taking place in Vietnam, the non-proliferation of nuclear arms treaty signed with the USSR had just come into force, a sign of eased relations between the East and the West that was good for business. The anti-conformist movement sweeping the world reached the mountains of Switzerland, too. Not only did the popular initiative looking to reduce "foreign influence" pass in 1970, but women also earned the right to federal votes a year later. On top of that, in May 1971, the European currency crisis led the Swiss National Bank to revalue the Swiss franc by 7.07% against the US dollar. This made Swiss currency a safe haven, even though it was still cheaper to borrow than any other European currency.

Geneva, Place du Lac: building for the First National City Bank, July 1970 [Atelier Boissonnas, CIG]

Citibank had to expand its business and finance a growing number of American companies expanding to Europe. Interested by the attractiveness of the Swiss franc, businessmen from across the Atlantic rushed through the bank's doors to borrow funds converted immediately into the European currency of their choice at a rate determined by Citibank! Since the 1960s, Swiss banks had seen a rising flow of foreign capital. This phenomenon continued into the 70s, much to several other European countries' chagrin. During the first three years of the 70s, Citibank alone lent almost a billion dollars to the large American companies that were setting up shop on the Old Continent. The American banking model was supporting the American business model! Thanks to the banks in general, and Citibank in particular, Europe began to slowly adopt technological progresses developed and commercialised in the United States.

Split between Zurich and Geneva, Jean-Pierre no doubt often looked out on the Seujet neighbourhood, just across from his Geneva offices. He had no way of knowing then that the reconstruction projects in that part of town the newspapers kept talking about would one day hold his own bank! But there was no time to worry about his future plans. At that time, he was busy setting up the business banking model he hoped would be developed.

AT THE BEGINNING

Jean-Pierre Cuoni during the 60s [Demole Archives]

> "The first element of this model was probably created at Citibank in 1972."
>
> Jean-Pierre Cuoni

In collaboration with Phillip Colebatch, an influential Australian member of Citibank who would later play a major role with Crédit Suisse, in 1972 Jean-Pierre took part in the creation of the Association of Foreign Banks in Switzerland AFBS. This brought together banks and other financial establishments held by a foreign shareholder and established in Switzerland. The new entity helped close ranks vis-à-vis the federal administration, the Swiss Association of Bankers and the other players in the financial centre[12].

Although Citibank was booming, the institution was doing everything it could to dominate market shares. For example, it set up throughout all of Europe the Marti financial management system (*machine de retranscription télex instantanée*, instantaneous telegraph retranscription machine), which sped up money transferring operations[13]. Jean-Pierre once again found himself facing another challenge coming from America.

In the summer of 1971, the Nixon administration decided to end the Bretton Woods system, which was too restrictive when it came to exchange rates[14]. At the same time, international trade had radically changed with the creation of the European Economic Community, which swept from the North Sea to the shores of the Mediterranean.

The Bretton Woods Agreement

The result of the Bretton Woods conference organised from 01 to 22 July 1944 in New Hampshire, the Bretton Woods Agreement laid out the provisions of the international financial system put in place following the Second World War. The United States' economic growth throughout the war and the amassing of American capital enabled Washington to promote a monetary system capable of providing a solid framework for the economic reconstruction and expansion of the "free world". The United States and the dollar found themselves as the pillars of the new economic structure. The conference created a Gold Exchange Standard based on the US dollar. All other currencies were now defined by the dollar, which itself was defined on gold. Two organisms were created at that time: the International Bank for Reconstruction and Development, known today as the World Bank, and the International Monetary Fund. The creation of the Euromarket spelled the end for the Bretton Woods Agreement, as some could obtain dollars without the oversight of the United States. From 200 million dollars in 1959, the Euromarket's uncontrolled monetary mass rose to 3 billion in 1961 and 46 billion in 1970. The amount of currency in circulation quickly outstripped the amount of total worldwide currency reserves, thus threatening global destabilisation.

JEAN-PIERRE CUONI, A BANKER WITH HEART

Geneva, pont des Bergues and quai Général-Guisan by night, second half of the 20th century [CIG]

The end of the Bretton Woods Agreement took place following a complicated period for the US economy. Although Citi was confident in the summer of 1970 that American company revenues would finally stop declining, bank specialists analysing the numbers given by some 1,400 company clients showed a decline in revenue at around 6% compared to the second quarter of 1969, reaching heights of 28% in the aerospace sector. Citi leadership was worried. They had strongly criticised the adoption of a new law in October 1970 putting in place heavy restrictions on imports into the United States. According to their economists, the new proposition set up the strictest measures against international trade since the passing of the infamous Smoot-Hawley law on custom tariffs in 1930. The decision raised fears of protectionism, which would lead to trade wars and inflation hikes[15]!

Richard Nixon announces the suspension of the convertibility of the dollar to gold in place since 1944, in August 1971 [Public domain]

Still, America beat to the tune of the General Electric Company, who leapt back from a deficit of 43 million dollars at the start of the year to a profit of 98 million dollars in the summer of 1970. Many at the time had high hopes for 1971[16]. That had to be how companies outside of the financial sector showing clear growth felt for the first few months of that year.

However, this fleeting upturn did nothing to dissuade the US Treasury from the decision it was about to make. By wiping out practically overnight the system that had guaranteed worldwide economic stability for more than 25 years, the Treasury profoundly transformed the international model. This brought with it a slew of both hopes and fears.

Private Banking

At that point, Jean-Pierre's business changed rapidly. The dollar was now floating, and in 1971 American clients were reimbursing loans in Swiss francs while taking out new ones in New York, Paris or Frankfort.

That was when Jean-Pierre Cuoni and his closest colleagues decided to modify their own business by grafting onto the Swiss private banking model, creating a new client base of wealthy individuals looking to place their money in Switzerland by starting a wealth management operation. It was a deft manoeuvre, one that was linked to the merchant origins of the old banking houses by operating through trading, a proven technique by then. At the same time, the political and economic stability of Switzerland was also a selling point. In doing so, Jean-Pierre dubbed his new business "Private Banking", as the role of "private banker" was protected. The name was now his, and it was one that other banking institutions would often adopt.

It was a tricky wager. The goal was to convince Citibank clients from around the world who held accounts in a Swiss bank to transfer their funds to Citibank's Swiss branch. To do so, Jean-Pierre hired a handful of people to be put throughout the Citi agency network, charged with enticing potential clients to come to Switzerland and drum up business. Although the results of this exercise would take a bit of time, they ended up being significant. While the business wasn't without its risks, of course, it had come at the right time. In the spring of 1972, the US economy broached another expansion phase, boosting the planet's markets and stock holdings while limiting inflation rates.

AT THE BEGINNING

> "We have a business which is highly stimulating from a growth perspective, and my mission in life, along with Lonnie, is to determine where to apply more capital and where to find and hire new people. It's stimulating, and it is fun."
>
> Jean-Pierre Cuoni

Jean-Pierre Cuoni in 1968 [Demole Archives]

By the end of 1972, the dollar's position had strengthened against the currencies of other industrial nations. Although the US trade deficit (at a yearly level of six billion dollars throughout the first ten months of 1972) was still high while waiting for the positive effects of the US currency's devaluation, the demand for American products was growing rapidly as business picked up again in Europe and in Japan[17]. For Jean-Pierre, the fog of uncertainty that global markets had fallen into for several months was lifting, giving glimpses of exciting prospects. At the same time in July 1972, as America, bogged down in a war since 1961, was launching Operation Linebacker, a massive bombardment campaign against North Vietnamese forces, Citibank had set up a new international commercial bank with an Asian partner, Fuji Bank Ltd. This new bank, seated in Hong-Kong and Singapore, was meant to service South-East Asia, Australia and the entire Pacific region under the name of Asia Pacific Capital Corporation Ltd (APCO)[18].

A few months later, in November, under the impetus of its CEO Walter Bigelow Wriston - who had just declined Nixon's offer to make him the new Secretary of the Treasury - Citi opened yet another new branch in the Sultanate of Brunei, the 91st country the bank had expanded to. They thereby introduced this small country to the beginnings of an American banking presence[19].

AT THE BEGINNING

Geneva, plaine de Plainpalais: protest against the Vietnam War, 21.04.1965 [CIG]

Medal crafted by Medallic Art Co. to commemorate the 150th anniversary (1812 to 1962) of the First City National Bank of New York. The large nude figure with its arms outstretched in a protective position represents the spirit of the American people. It is surrounded by figures representing Family, Culture, Trade, Transport, Industry and Agriculture. [Public domain]

At the end of 1972, Citibank was still expanding widely. A year later, it granted a loan of 200 million dollars to Pertamina, an Indonesian state oil company[20]. This was just before Max A. Fischer was named Citi's head of industrial banking. Based in Zurich, he had worked for the bank since 1963 and had been in charge of the World Corporation Group in Switzerland[21], working often with Jean-Pierre. In 1975, Citi opened another branch in Copenhagen, becoming the first bank to have branches in all nine countries in the Common Market[22]. There was a small revolution in February 1976: First National City Bank changed its named to Citibank.

Having acted as head of wealth management for Europe, the Middle East and Africa, Jean-Pierre was named Chairman of Citibank-Switzerland. It was a tumultuous period. In 1978, Citi had announced that it would no longer lend money to South Africa, in protest against the policy of Apartheid. This decision led other American banking institutions to review their stance towards South Africa[23].

> Citi's position was notable, as it was an early intervention in the reform process that was just beginning in South Africa. It wouldn't be until 1984 under President Pieter Botha that a new constitution creating a three-chamber parliament would be set in place; all the while, Western pressure and economic measures against the country strengthened. Apartheid laws would not be abolished until the end of the 1980s.

These were years of bitter work, where Jean-Pierre found his strength in his loved ones, especially his wife and his daughter.

Yet though his private life was calm, he was soon to face problems from across the Atlantic.

The Cuoni family in 1975
[Demole Archives]

Jean-Pierre and Yvonne Cuoni, the Seventies [Demole Archives]

In the early 1980s, Citibank was in the spotlight following revelations that led the US Federal Securities and Exchange Commission to open an investigation starting in 1978. The investigation revealed that from 1973 to 1980, thousands of suspicious operations had been carried out, operations that bordered legality. Censured by several countries, Citi was forced to pay some 11 million dollars in fines and back taxes, even though the U.S. considered that these practices were not of such nature as to allow for prosecution of the bank. Still, the crisis rattled the institution even as far away as Switzerland, where one-third of profits generated by affiliates of the bank had been transferred to an affiliate in Nassau, where taxes rates were much lower[24]. Far removed from these events, Jean-Pierre would still explain later that certain aspects forced a weighing up of interests and ethical choices that would brand the person making them.

"Throughout my career, I've had to make some very difficult decisions. Once, one of my clients, a prominent person from a country going through a revolution, was imprisoned. A third party had demanded that I transfer a giant sum of money to liberate him, otherwise my client would be executed. I was completely on my own at that point. Should I try to discuss it with my client? Impossible, he was in prison. Ask for my boss's opinion? He couldn't take on that responsibility for me. I decided to pay, without any guarantees it would work. Luckily, my client was freed"[25].

Jean-Pierre Cuoni

Despite these challenges, at the end of 1982 Citi became America's largest bank, outstripping even the prestigious Bank of America. That same year, Citi spread out even further in Switzerland, creating the Citicorp Bank in Zurich. This new entity took on all of Geneva's Citicorp International Finance's activities, including private banking and management operations which Jean-Pierre took with him[26]. Jean-Pierre was to return yet again to Zurich as Senior Vice-Chairman of the new establishment. He would soon be named as well Vice-Chairman of the Association of Foreign Banks in Switzerland, working with Ernst F. Schaad, chairman of the association as well as Director General of Nat West[27].

Jean-Pierre Cuoni during the 1970s [Demole Archives]

Prime Tower, Zurich, seat of Citibank in Switzerland [Public domain]

Citigroup Center, Lexington Avenue, Manhattan [@Tdorante10, Public domain]

> Citibank in Zurich moved to Hardstrasse 201 in 2012, settling into the iconic Prime Tower dominating the city at 126 metres tall.

The 80s was a decade of revolution and extraordinary technological progress, all under the direction of a conservative-leaning neoliberalism championed by US President Ronald Reagan and British Prime Minister Margaret Thatcher. While Europe was uniting into a single market within the European Economic Community, the bipolar world was slowly coming to an end as the USSR reformed and the Berlin Wall famously fell on 10 November 1989. In 1984 in Switzerland, the public rejected the popular initiative "against the abuse of banking secrecy and power", reaffirming banks' freedom in their activities. The referendum, however, did not ward off the crisis that would spring up to shake the world three years later. Those mechanisms had already been triggered long before that. Already in 1979, the US Federal Reserve had sharply increased interest rates to combat inflation, causing a severe recession and a gradual inflow of capital into the United States, thereby increasing the value of the dollar to its level before 1971. Risks of instability were growing too high. As such, the G7 countries met in New York in September 1985 to agree on a market intervention for exchange rates and to depreciate the value of the dollar. Economic flows were going to work. Too well, even, as in 1987 the same countries met again during the Louvre Accord to slow down the lowering of the dollar. Still, the effects were too pronounced for the US domestic economy, as the stock markets were skyrocketing. This generated inflation tensions as well as an unavoidable rise in interest rates with the signature of the Louvre Accord. Developments picked up during the summer before rising to a fever pitch in the autumn, provoking on 19 October the largest stock market crash since 1929. This new "Black Monday" saw the Dow Jones drop by 508 points after 600 million shares were transferred via automatic computer software, programmed to sell any shares or bonds once the market reached a critical level. Investors lost 600 billion dollars, and the planet witnessed an almost instant collapse of the entire stock market. The event proved Walter Wriston, CEO of Citicorp at the beginning of the 80s, right. He had postulated that information about money had become as valuable as money itself, as safes had in the end been replaced by computers.

Iran, 1973 [Demole Archives]

A new era

"When you gamble, the point isn't participating, it's winning."
Jean-Pierre Cuoni

Jean-Pierre Cuoni was to leave Citi not long after. Did these events play a role in his decision? Perhaps. Whatever the reason, the "serial entrepreneur" felt himself stagnating and had a growing need for change. Most of all, he was confronted with the growing jealousy of several bankers who envied the developments in Private Banking that he had dedicated so much effort to. Pressure was at its highest in 1984, to the extent that he even considered quitting to join Bank Leu. However, the Board of Directors did not allow him the opportunity, refusing his resignation. As a result, he did not hesitate once offered the chance to manage the Handelsbank National Westminster Bank (Natwest) in 1988. The challenge was far too attractive. He had already been able to evaluate all the promises the institution offered by sidling up to Ernst F. Schaad within the Association for Foreign Banks in Switzerland.

Just after leaving, Jean-Pierre witnessed another scandal that shook Citi. This time it was a matter of fraud committed by the former Vice-Prime Minister of Greece, M. Koutsogiorgas, who had diverted almost 200 million dollars of laundered funds through Citicorp[28]. He was also taken aback by the duplicity of one of Citicorp's private banking clients, Asil Nadir, the CEO of the British company Polly Peck. Nadir had diverted more than 150 million pounds sterling from his company and had been condemned to 10 years imprisonment[29].

Protected from these cases, Jean-Pierre was in the process of creating an international private bank on behalf of Handelsbank Natwest by taking over Coutts Bank.

David Burdett Money-Coutts (1931-2012) was a descendant of the founder of Coutts bank, Thomas Coutts, and a grandson of Lord Latymer. An English Tory and a former dragoon for His Majesty, having served in Germany and Egypt, he was also a hussar in the Royal Gloucestershire Hussars TA. David Money-Coutts became one of the pillars of family banking after 1954 and was a well-known figure in the City of London. He was all the more well known for having pushed his bank into the future by adopting one of the first electric accounting systems in 1963. In 1970, Money-Coutts was named Executive Director of the institution; six years later he was appointed as Chairman. In 1991, he was made Chairman again of the new Coutts & Co Group, before finally retiring from business in 1996.

The Coutts Group fell into the hands of the Royal Bank of Scotland in 2000 with the takeover of International Westminster Bank. In 2015, the Royal Bank of Scotland then resold Coutts & Co Ltd's private banking and international wealth management activities to Union Bancaire Privée.

He would remain the *Chief Executive Officer* for four years under the chairmanship of Sir David Money-Coutts[30]. The creation was very much in the spirit of the times in the United Kingdom. Founded in 1692, the time-honoured Coutts & Co was the eighth-oldest bank in the world. It had already merged with Westminster Bank in 1969, and in 1987 furthered its international appeal by moving to Geneva. In October 1990, Coutts and NatWest decided to strengthen their international image by creating the Coutts Group via their different affiliates.

Throughout his years as head of Coutts Bank Switzerland, Jean-Pierre pushed the bank to rare heights of excellence and performance. In doing so, he made the bank one of the largest foreign banks in Switzerland in the 21st century, with 1,300 employees managing 36.6 billion francs by the end of 2013[31]. However, in 1994, several bad investments were made while Jean-Pierre was on holiday. That had to have clicked with him, or even have been a source of inspiration!

Sir David Money-Coutts
[Public domain]

[Demole Archives]

A NEW ERA

EFG Private Bank

"We put the client at the center, and for that you have to put the CRO at the center."

Jean-Pierre Cuoni

In 1995, after three decades of hard work, determination and experience, a new adventure began.

At 50 years old, Jean-Pierre dove into a huge new project with the help of one of his friends, Lawrence Howell, as well as the encouragement of his wife, Yvonne. Creating a new bank required skills, a strong heart and a heavy dose of courage. Both Jean-Pierre and Lawrence had all of these ingredients in heaps!

"Lonnie" was a long-time travel companion. The two men had met in 1979 in Switzerland at Citibank[33]. They had been inseparable since. Lonnie often told Jean-Pierre *"Everything I know, I learned it from you"*.

"After 35 years as a wealth manager, I wanted to found a new bank. On the one hand I had my own skills, and on the other I had a top-notch professional network that I had built throughout my career"[32].

Jean-Pierre Cuoni

Jean-Pierre Cuoni and Lawrence Howell [Demole Archives]

At the end of the 70s, Lawrence Howell acted as an internal legal advisor for Citi before being appointed as head for Europe, the Middle East and Africa in 1981. After a short stint with McKinsey & Co from 1984 to 1985, Lonnie came back to the fold as Vice-Chairman in charge of ultra-high net worth Swiss clients at Citibank Switzerland. This reunited him with Jean-Pierre, who was already thinking of leaving Citi.

In 1989, he followed Jean-Pierre, his mentor, to Zurich to join Coutts & Co. There, he was responsible for the bank's Americas and Asia sector, managing clients residing in the Americas as well as all the bank's offices in the United States, the Bahamas, Bermuda, the Cayman Islands and in Latin America.

Lawrence Howell [Public domain]

"To found EFG, Mr Cuoni invested his "pension money," about three million francs, as did Mr Howell, and the two persuaded Spiro Latsis to invest the rest of the 24 million Swiss francs in seed capital"

"Entrepreneurial Banker Uses Crisis to Consolidate",
The New York Times, 2009.

In 1995, the two men decided to create a new entity, managing to convince the man that would later become a major partner, John Spyridon Latsis. In 1979, Latsis had bought from Onassis Banque de Dépôts in Geneva, which had been founded in 1929. Banque de Dépôts had CHF 776,068[34] in equity funds in 1995. While Jean-Pierre and Lonnie were becoming its main actors, Jean-Pierre was quickly named a director of the institution. The first decision was to open that same year a branch of Banque de Dépôts in Zurich, one exclusively dedicated to wealth management. At the same time, an affiliate was opened in Miami, BDD Capital International.

With Lonnie, Jean-Pierre brought Marcus Caduff, Mats Pehrsson, Esther Heer and Thomas Muther (whom Jean-Pierre had known since the beginning of his career at Citi) into his new venture, along with five other trusted bankers. The first task was to find a site. 16 Bahnhofstrasse in Zurich was quickly chosen[35]. The second task was to furnish the offices. As it happens, a bank had just closed in Zurich, which was the perfect opportunity to collect desks, chairs, coffee-makers and staplers[36].

[Demole Archives]

> "Jean Pierre's immense courage and vision, his enthusiasm to motivate a leadership team, and his ability to adjust to market changes all contributed to the successful IPO of the business he founded. Undoubtedly, these are also the qualities that made him both an exemplary leader and a role model for those who had the privilege to work alongside him. The title "Banker with Heart" best describes his love of people in general, of the customer and the business team. By being a good listener, he earned their respect and commitment. On a personal note, I valued the qualities that extended far beyond his professional life – his unwavering love of his family, his humor and his generosity. I admired him for his balanced leadership and continue to cherish our longstanding friendship."
>
> Guenther Greiner

EFG Bank opened its doors on 01 September 1995, with very little resources. Although the first months were challenging, Jean-Pierre never faltered.

Jean-Pierre quickly inspired the same levels of goodwill and ambition in everyone. He was someone who could talk to both carpenters and statesmen, a charming, charismatic man who was a skilful persuader and ever-encouraging to the people he was close to. He even organised the office Christmas parties. He was "always on the dance floor", according to one of his former partners[37]! He let his Lucerne roots shine through on every occasion, eating Wiener Schnitzel every now and then at the Old Swiss House. Yet in spite of the extraordinary energy that pushed him past his limits every day, Jean-Pierre would confess a few years later that:

> "I stopped working in 1995."
>
> Jean-Pierre Cuoni

Anyone who saw him knew that that was debatable. For Jean-Pierre had such a passion for his company that he didn't feel he was working; however, his dedication to his work often kept him behind his desk until late at night, even on Saturdays and Sundays. And then the office, the registers and the business meetings in a relaxed Swiss atmosphere was only one aspect of the business that he devoted his time to. Jean-Pierre also spent a great deal of time on airlines.

> Nos chargés de clientèle ont leur propre stratégie. Nous n'avons ni segmentation, ni répartition géographique, ni seuils d'entrée.
> **Jean-Pierre Cuoni**

Abu Dhabi [Public domain]

His travels took him across six continents, meeting all sorts of new people who were often curious and always shocked by his bravado, coming all the way from Europe. Jean-Pierre often found himself in colourful situations. For example, once at a meal in the Far East, he had to taste a spoonful of monkey brains without making a face to avoid insulting his hosts. At another dinner in the Middle East, he was served a still-warm sheep's heart. However, this was a culinary honour he subtly passed on to the unfortunate colleague there with him[38]!

Although some business trips were without a doubt a bit funny, such as his refusal to take off his shoes in front of in front of a Far Eastern potentate, others were more dramatic. Once, a coup d'état took place on the other side of a door in the antechamber where Jean-Pierre was waiting for a meeting, unaware of the events unfolding. Another time he was mugged coming out of a taxi; however, he escaped by overpowering his armed attacker, whom he managed to lose by hiding under an emergency staircase in a dark alleyway.

His long experience in Private Banking in the United States, Switzerland and with numerous clients, as much during his travels as behind his desk, enabled Jean-Pierre to think of new ways of doing something. It was an original operation that no one had ever dared put in place, something that he, along with Lonnie, was going to develop for Banque de Dépôts: the idea of a partnership with the employees.

As a result, Lonnie and Jean-Pierre started hiring based on their new model, one Jean-Pierre had been thinking of for a long time. It would shake up all of the Swiss banking industry. In doing so, Jean-Pierre involved his employees to the highest degree, granting them 34% of the group's share capital. In any case, he refused over the years to use the term "employee", calling them his partners instead.

> "I want to talk to entrepreneurs, not employees. That's our model!"[39]
>
> Jean-Pierre Cuoni

What weren't people in the field saying? The new model seemed crazy, outlandish, even bizarre. The critiques were flying. "Courage and belief!" Jean-Pierre took these core values to heart[40] throughout the development of his business model, ignoring the rants and scathing comments tied up in the traditions of a vertical hierarchy.

> "Creating EFG, in 1994 Lonnie and I had about 50 years of private banking experience and what we did know then is how not to do it. A bank that is completely client-oriented. We say the closeness to our client is the most important thing. Thus, our CRO must be at the center as they are close to the client, they own the client. Most banks haven't understood this. We tell them: your clients are yours. Our bank doesn't have clients, it has CROs. And the CROs have clients. There's a big difference. CROs act in the interest of the clients, we do not force our CROs to sell anything, we want them to be advisors. Make tailor-made advice to the client they know as they know better than the CEO and managers of the bank what the client's interests are. That is the basic model we use and that is why we have been growing faster in the market than any other banks in the past years. This model leads to the motivation CROs have to be enormous."
>
> Jean-Pierre Cuoni

The new model was winning, as its first success didn't take long. In 1996, Banque de Dépôts took over the Luxembourg group Consolidated Eurofinance Holdings. As the company also belonged to the Latsis family, it was a risk-free operation; still, it was also a sizeable one. Consolidated Eurofinance Holdings was actually a powerful holding combining The Private Bank and Trust Company Ltd in London, The Private Bank and Trust Company Ltd in Guernsey, Euromerchant Bank SA in Greece, Interbank Hellas in Athens and its 22 branches, as well as Banque de Dépôts SA in Luxembourg. The merger under the Geneva bank increased Banque de Dépôt's accounts at the end of June 1996 to 880 million francs for a total of 1,200 people.

It was during these years that Jean-Pierre attended the World Economic Forum in Davos, for more than twenty years.

> "At EFG, everyone was responsible for his or her clients, as well as his or her revenues, as they depended on each person's results."
>
> Lawrence Howell

Jean-Pierre then explained that the consolidation was one of the main reasons for the restructuring. In any case, the newly-created group was going to open a branch in Geneva under Jean-Pierre's exclusive supervision, playing a role as a holding company.

This was how European Financial Group EFG was born. Its first task was to coordinate activities from the various group branches in Geneva, Zurich, London, Guernsey, Luxembourg, Miami, Sao Paulo and Monaco[41].

The banking activities were going very strong. At the same time, however, troubles were brewing in the field. On the one hand, there was the Salinas scandal, involving the brother of the Mexican president Carlos Salinas de Gortari, who held funds in Citi. Citi was cleared of charges following an investigation by the US General Accounting Office and a Senate hearing. On the other hand, there was the issue of unclaimed assets.

> Commemorations for the end of the Second World War took place in 1995, resulting in historic demands: the reimbursement of funds belonging to Jewish Holocaust victims lying in unclaimed accounts. An investigatory committee was organised in 1996. Called the Independent Committee of Eminent Persons (or the "Volcker Commission"), the committee was chaired by Paul Volcker, a former chair of the American Federal Reserve, and aimed to investigate banks, especially Swiss ones. At the same time, the Federal Council appointed an independent commission of experts, the "Bergier Commission", charged with putting the spotlight on Switzerland's position during WWII[42].

Of course, European Financial Group EFG had nothing to do with these shades from the past. Wealth management was doing better than ever, in spite of the economic recession following the 1987 crash that was still affecting the world. Still, China's phenomenal development and the slow opening of the former Soviet Union, which had begun its swan song as the Berlin Wall fell eight years earlier, created a solid, diverse base for the field.

In April 1997, Jean-Pierre and Lonnie, still in partnership with the Latsis family, bought the Royal Bank of Scotland affiliate in Zurich, with the company name of EFG Private Bank SA. That meant that European Financial Group EFG now held, with the Private Bank and Trust Company, two of the jewels of British banking.

The group held at that point a total capital of 950 million francs and a balance sheet sum of 5 billion, proof of its excellence[43].

In September of the same year, Banque de Dépôts de Genève changed its name. It now operated under the name of EFG Bank European Financial Group, under the tutorship of the European Financial Group, which turned into EFG Bank Group at the same time[44].

In 1997, Jean-Pierre had succeeded in installing his new model, and the criticism had morphed into praise. That was something he would remember for the rest of his life. His sunny personality and his love of life helped him quickly forget the rants and the jabs. What's more, the model he had worked so painstakingly to develop was a real success. He would even say it himself a few years later[45].

> "Bringing together, as we did, a team of highly-experienced, business-minded bankers. Make everyone a stakeholder, invested in our success. Grant them the independence needed to respond to their clients' needs with as little bureaucracy and as much creativity as possible. Eliminate conflicts of interest."
>
> Jean-Pierre Cuoni

This was how he rebuilt Banque Scandinave, as well as Banque Edouard Constant that had succeeded the former in 1997 and that merged with EFG Private Bank in 2003. He hopped from success to success, with support from his wife, Yvonne, who informed her husband every morning of changes in the stock market or important worldwide current events. By the end of the 90s, Jean-Pierre had made EFG a reference in the field.

> "Taking part isn't important, you need to win!"
>
> Jean-Pierre Cuoni

A NEW ERA

Monsieur
Jean-Pierre Cuoni

Si l'idéal de la Suisse ouverte sur le monde pouvait s'incarner, il aurait votre visage.

Homme d'écoute et de décision, vous êtes de ceux qui ont donné lustre et considération au métier de banquier en Suisse. Votre perception du monde et de vos concitoyens — Alémanique parmi les Alémaniques, Romand parmi les Romands — ont fait de vous un banquier soucieux de l'avenir de sa profession et du pays.

Sans intérêt pour le futile, concentré sur le progrès, vous savez saisir l'instant de concilier. Ainsi votre action au Comité de l'Association suisse des banquiers a-t-elle été dominée par la recherche efficace du dialogue, par la fidélité aux engagements convenus et par un soutien sans faille aux intérêts généraux communs.

J'ai aimé travailler avec vous et je me réjouis que ce bref hommage m'offre l'occasion de vous le dire, en vous souhaitant un

Heureux Anniversaire !

Jean-Paul Chapuis

Bâle, 7 juillet 1997

Letter from Jean-Paul Chapuis, General Secretary of the Swiss Association of Bankers
[Demole Archives]

Zurich, August 8, 1997
HJB/ez

Dear Jean Pierre,

On the occasion of your 60th Birthday I hasten to send you – somewhere at sea – our very best Birthday Wishes.

We have travelled the international banking road together for many, many years and I was sad when finally our ways parted. You were my eternal mentor, especially during our years on the board of the Swiss Bankers Association. After you left, life was never the same!

I would like to thank you for the decades of good friendship, and I look forward to an early reunion to celebrate your 60th on *terra firma*.

Sincerely,

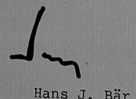

Hans J. Bär

Letter from Hans Julius Bär, representative of Swiss banks during the 90s and a member of the Volcker Commission looking into unclaimed funds of victims of Nazism [Demole Archives]

Into the new millennium, EFG, and more particularly EFG Private Bank – the Swiss private bank of EFG Bank Group – would see its profits rise substantially year after year. In 2000, EFG introduced itself to Asian markets by opening a representative and broker/dealer office in Hong Kong, as well as a representative and an investment advice office in Singapore, each becoming affiliates in 2002 and 2003, respectively. In 2001, EFG acquired IBP Fondkommission. Net profits after tax rose by 43% in 2003, up to 33 million. At the same time, client assets rose by 120% to 20 billion by the end of the year, thanks to acquisitions and natural growth. In 2003, EFG Private Bank counted more than 550 employers around the world. The institution created by Jean-Pierre also benefited from the acquisition of BanSabadell Finance, and especially from the merger with and integration of Banque Edouard Constant. The latter represented one of the key drivers of business and exceptional results in the period[46].

> "With Asia remaining the single largest area of organic growth, EFG continued its investment in the region by opening a branch office in Singapore. In Scandinavia the Bank benefited from rebounding market trends. The Miami subsidiary, which serves Latin America, experienced a significant business growth. Good results were achieved in asset management by deploying increasingly alternative investments products. The combination of low credit risk and high asset quality has led to a credit portfolio with no losses to date. The most significant event in 2003 was the merger with the Geneva-based Banque Edouard Constant, which added CHF 6.5 billion to the growth of clients' funds. The integration of BEC was accomplished to a large degree by year-end. Due to the merger, EFG will become a member of the Swiss Stock Exchanges, SWX and VIRT-X."
>
> Press release – EFG Private Bank, 16 March 2004

A NEW ERA

Communiqué de presse – Zurich-Genève / Suisse, le 27 mai 2003

→ (Ne peut être publié avant le 27 mai 2003 à 15h00)

EFG Private Bank SA et Banque Edouard Constant SA décident de fusionner

EFG Private Bank SA (EFG) et Banque Edouard Constant SA (BEC), basées à Zurich et Genève, toutes deux spécialisées dans les métiers de la banque privée et de la gestion de patrimoines, ont décidé de fusionner à fin juin de cette année.

La nouvelle entité bancaire issue de cette fusion comprendra environ 500 employés, CHF 17 milliards de fonds de la clientèle sous gestion et des revenus de l'ordre de CHF 200 millions. Elle sera géographiquement représentée aussi bien sur le plan international qu'au travers de la Suisse, avec des bureaux à Genève, Lausanne, Zurich et en Valais, ainsi qu'à Hong Kong, Singapour, Taiwan, Monaco, Guernsey, Miami, Buenos Aires, Stockholm, Malmö, Göteborg et Helsinki.

Compte tenu de sa taille et de son positionnement international, le nom EFG Private Bank SA a été retenu pour la nouvelle entreprise fusionnée. Cette dernière fera partie de EFG Bank Group dont le total des fonds propres s'élève à CHF 3.2 milliards. La Fondation de Famille Sandoz demeurera actionnaire minoritaire de la nouvelle entité et sera représentée au Conseil d'administration.

Monsieur Cuoni, Président du CA de EFG Private Bank SA, relève que : « l'aggrégation des capacités et tailles de ces deux institutions positionnera effectivement la nouvelle banque dans les premiers rangs des banques privées, tant en Suisse que sur le plan international, en termes de service à la clientèle, d'innovation de produits et de présence géographique. Nous avons l'intention de poursuivre le développement dynamique de notre établissement par un effort permanent visant à offrir à nos clients un service nous positionnant parmi les meilleurs de la branche».

Cette transaction est sujette à l'obtention de l'accord formel de la Commission Fédérale des Banques, autorité de surveillance.

EFG Private Bank a utilisé pour cette transaction les conseils de Lehman Brothers, La Fondation de Famille Sandoz ceux de Goldman Sachs International.

Personnes de contact :

Pour EFG
Jean-Pierre Cuoni, Président du
Conseil d'Administration
EFG Private Bank SA

Pour BEC
Pascal Dubey, Responsable
Marketing & Communication
Banque Edouard Constant SA

Pour la Fondation de Famille Sandoz
Jörg Denzler, porte-parole
Sandoz - Fondation de Famille

In 2004, EFG acquired as well Banco Atlántico Gibraltar Ltd, followed by the acquisition of six private banking entities over the following two years, i.e. EFG Private Bank Ltd, a sister company based in London, EFG Eurofinancière d'investissements SAM, a second sister company based in Monaco, as well as Dresdner Lateinamerika Financial Advisors LLC in Miami, Banco Sabadell's private banking activities in the Bahamas, Chiltern Wealth Management in London, Bank von Ernst (Liechtenstein) AG and Capital Management Advisor Ltd. in Bermuda.

Entering the stock exchange

But it wasn't until 2005 that EFG would get the lion's share when the bank entered the stock exchange, ten years to the date after its creation. It had been a real marathon to reach that point, and Jean-Pierre had not held back! He had had to carry out a number of preparatory steps, including modifying the accounting methods of the Swiss GAAP standards to the IFRS standards, which required devoted work from more than one technician. Above all else, in October 2005, the bank launched an Initial Public Offering (IPO), open to the public and underwritten seven times. It was comprised of 36,670,000 new shares on the SWX Swiss Exchange. The operation set records, not only because it was the fastest entry into the stock exchange in Swiss banking history, but also because it brought in 1.39 billion in new capital.

> "A private bank without equal."
>
> Jean-Pierre Cuoni

Banque Assurance
Le magazine des professionnels de la finance et de l'assurance

5/03 Septembre/Octobre 2003 CHF 11.- EUR 8.65

Président d'EFG
Jean-Pierre Cuoni
L'AMBITIEUX

PRIVATE BANKING: AVALANCHE DE CRITIQUES

De nombreux rapports et un message identique: les banques continuent à travailler comme avant. Elles peinent à tirer les conséquences des évolutions récentes et à adapter de nouveaux comportements. Analyse et propositions.

Ackermann provoque la polémique

Les idées du patron de la Deutsche Bank pour les banques allemandes.

La devise de Rolf Dörig

Le nouveau CEO de la Renten veut revenir à une politique conservatrice.

Les assurances doivent mieux communiquer

Tel est le credo d'Albert Lauper. Grande interview du nouveau président de l'ASA.

> "Our service at EFG Bank is equal to none. This is a statement that I know but cannot prove in front of you today. I can only invite you to come, use us, and find it out."
>
> Jean-Pierre Cuoni

Their success was undeniable, a success to which Yvonne had largely contributed, which Jean-Pierre celebrated to the tinkling of flutes of Ruinart Blanc de Blancs. While some trembled at the thought of it, others were ecstatic. Upon entering the stock exchange, EFG handled almost 27,000 clients around the world, whose assets amounted to over CHF 47 billion. This included shares held on deposit, fiduciary investments, deposits, client loans, funds, investment funds under management, third party funds and structured products. The number of employees had grown as well, doubling in two years to 1,053 employees[47]. That same year, Lonnie would acknowledge this again[48].

> "Client Relationship Officers are still being drawn to EFG. They're interested by our approach, which lets them manage their business as if the bank belongs to them. This kind of individual delegation of power is rare, and is the cornerstone of our international banking organisation."
>
> Lawrence Howell

Throughout the following year, in 2006, EFG opened new offices in Dubai, Bahrein, Djakarta, Mexico, Caracas, Bogotá and Quito. It also started banking operations in Luxembourg and in the Bahamas, all the while carrying out acquisitions such as Harris Allday, a stock broker for private clients in Great Britain, Banque Monégasque de Gestion in Monaco, Quesada Kapitalförvaltning AB in Sweden and C.M. Advisors Limited, based in Bermuda.

To top it all off, the bank dropped the name EFG Private Bank in February and retained EFG Bank instead, while creating the holding company EFG International, the new parent company of EFG Bank and all other subsidiaries, in a demerger process under Swiss law. In 2007, EFG took centre-stage again by buying Ashby London Financial Services Ltd.

> "EFG financial products provides the best transparency which helps you translate the products you buy for your clients in their portfolio. Through that fully automated term sheet we have, and it does work. Never should CROs be short of a translation when a client ask you what the hell do I have in my portfolio'. We provide security. No nostro trading, no risk taking, no owned positions, we have no fowl assets in our books and we have the capital. We are here to stay. We are a secure bank from an issuer risk point of view. And of course, we provide the sufficient liquidity for our financial products (200% liquidity) as they are all listed, every single one. We don't have a single position which is not listed."
>
> Jean-Pierre Cuoni

In a little over 10 years, and despite tense times brewing at the beginning of the new century, Jean-Pierre had built a real international empire with the help of Lonnie and a close circle of friends. Vice-President of the British Chamber of Commerce and a frequent attendee of the World Economic Forum in Davos since assuming his duties with Coutts, Jean-Pierre, while knowing how to remain discreet, had become a reference in the world of finance.

The early 2000s, however, were dominated by many major issues, from international commerce to energy resources and global warming. What's more, the world was still under threat from rising insecurity, with waves of more and more frequent terrorism often crippling the stock market. The fall of the Twin Towers in New York in 2001, which shocked Jean-Pierre, stunned the entire planet. The war that followed provoked economic shifts that were only fanned by China's phenomenal economic growth. In 2006, however, the outlook was excellent, not just for

EFG but for the entire banking industry. That year, UBS announced a record profit of CHF 14 billion for the year before, making it one of the world's leading banks. Likewise, Crédit Suisse announced a profit of CHF 5.85 billion. Few could have felt the disaster coming, one that had been nursed by years of financial deregulation. This led to a growing securitisation of financial products, up until the dramatic subprime crisis that began in July 2007 with the mortgage crash[49] in the United States and gradual freeze of financial relations between banks. Many still remember Lehman Brothers' shocking declaration of bankruptcy in September 2008. In regards to this, on 25 April 2008, the chairman of the Swiss National Bank, Jean-Pierre Roth, said, *"Banking risk measurement and management tools have been overtaken by a crisis that was originally limited to US mortgage markets. [We must] draw the consequences of banks' limited ability to measure their risks and authorities' limited ability to oversee them"*[50].

At first, EFG didn't report any considerable losses, only indicating impacts on assets under management and on the business of clients whose fears were managed by CROs as best they could[51]. In spring of 2008, just as EFG had acquired Marble Bar Asset Management LLP, a leading alternative asset manager in the UK, aftershocks from the credit markets hit several of the bank's clients due to Akos's declaration of bankruptcy. Akos was an investment fund managed by a Stockholm team that EFG had been selling to its institutional clients since 2004[52]. With all losses wiped, EFG weathered the crisis without any issues while Switzerland carried out measures to ensure UBS's financial stability, which had been hugely impacted.

EFG was also spared a few months later from the disastrous effects of the Madoff case, as "it had no exposure in its own name to any fund managed or advised by Madoff"[53]. However, as a precautionary measure, the bank put in place safeguards against potential losses for loans over 15 million Swiss francs, that is under 2% of total revenues.

Despite the general panic, Jean-Pierre was able to stay calm and optimistic[54] in face of one of the largest financial scams of the century, about which books would soon be written.

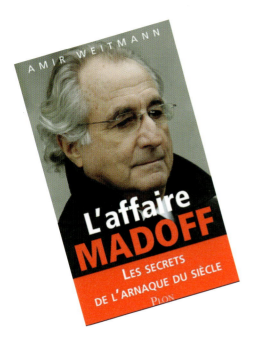

"It would not be an exaggeration to say that 2008 was one of the hardest years we've ever seen on an economic and financial basis. We witnessed volatile markets in free fall, well-known banks collapsing and strong concerns for liquidity, credit quality and the strength of capital in the entire banking sector. Various financial scandals have also increased the loss of confidence in financial services, while the real economy quickly entered into global recession during the last few months of the past year. We will come out of this crisis stronger than before and with an even better reputation."

Jean-Pierre Cuoni

And the bank did maintain its reputation. Still, "*There's no doubt that the past few years have been extremely difficult for the world economy*"[55]. The economic somersaults of the 2000s were to be replaced by yet another problem for many Swiss banks. In 2009, the Obama administration targeted Switzerland, and UBS in particular, by investigating through the Department of Justice or the IRS alleged tax evasion by some US companies. With the pressure growing too strong, FINMA, the Swiss Financial Market Supervisory Authority, quickly allowed UBS to provide 250 names to save its banking licence in the United States. We all know what happened next. UBS paid a fine of over 80 million dollars and was forced to provide 4,500 additional client names to the US authorities. With new US laws passed in 2010, Switzerland was forced to negotiate a new tax treaty with the United States, resulting in the loss of Swiss banking secrecy[56].

An eternal optimist, Jean-Pierre was not ready to give up, despite the exceptional times. How could the Americans, whom he had so admired, treat Swiss banking institutions like this[57]?

JEAN-PIERRE CUONI, A BANKER WITH HEART

However, EFG was not penalised the same way as many other Swiss banks. Once again, Jean-Pierre was quick to give a reassuring and hopeful speech, as he always did[58].

As a sign of the bank's strength, EFG moved its Zurich office in the fourth quarter of 2013, leaving its historic location on Bahnhofstrasse to move to a high-end building at Bleicherweg 8, near Paradeplatz, in the heart of Zurich's financial quarter. Jean-Pierre inaugurated the new office with his habitual modesty, but also with the satisfaction of watching his work become a reference not only in finance but also in Switzerland.

"I've already brought up the pressures that Switzerland faces as a financial centre, and I'm happy that a balanced solution, based on double taxation deal negotiations and a heightened collaboration with foreign authorities in tax evasion matters, could be found while respecting banking secrecy. As a result, recent events have shown that Switzerland's attractiveness comes from many factors, not just the tax aspect. Our country is stable socially and politically, has a solid economy and strong public finances and our financial services sector can rely on a vast wealth of know-how, highly-qualified professionals and a reputation for quality that has been known for a while. In my opinion, these factors give Switzerland a strong competitive advantage, which should support the country's attractiveness in the long term".

Jean-Pierre Cuoni

JEAN-PIERRE CUONI, A BANKER WITH HEART

A Philanthropic Ideal

The qualities Jean-Pierre brought up in his 2011 speech, as in many others for that matter, were the ones he had instilled in his bank for years. He represented quiet strength and unwavering optimism. He relied on loyalty, courage and work; he was a peerless orator gifted with a great deal of confidence and gusto when faced with people in power. He was a real banker with heart! He managed to transfer his own goodwill to his bank by involving it in a long-lasting philanthropic scheme.

It was his idea, and he did everything to put it in place. What cause did he choose? Children, primarily. Jean-Pierre involved EFG in a cause that was particularly important to him, deciding to support Right to Play, an international humanitarian organisation that provided aid to the neediest children on the planet.

"Let's go for it"

[Demole Archives]

[Demole Archives]

[Demole Archives]

Based on the belief that sport has the power to help make children happy and healthy, EFG's sustained commitment was to support communities in the most underprivileged regions of the world by using sports and activity programmes to encourage physical, social and emotional development of young people at risk, such as refugees, children impacted by war or orphans affected by the AIDS virus.

Obviously, many professional and Olympic athletes, like the Norwegian speed skater Johann Olav Koss, participated in Right to Play's efforts, *"acting as ambassadors for the cause, but also as role models for the children themselves."*

Jean-Pierre defended this cause against all odds by protecting, educating and developing in these young people the principle of autonomy. He was to ensure the vice-presidency of the organisation in Switzerland as well as of its international organ in Toronto.

In 2022, more than two million children and adolescents benefit or have benefited from the Right To Play programme.

Jean-Pierre had an optimistic outlook on EFG's support for Genève-Servette Hockey Club, with which a partnership was formed in 2007. Support was also given to sailing sports, particularly for the Société Nautique de Genève.

> "Learn, earn, return."
>
> Jean-Pierre Cuoni

EFG International is the main sponsor of Sailing Arabia The Tour since 2013 [sailingarabiatheto ur.com/archives]

However, it was undoubtedly the support his bank gave to music, especially jazz, that particularly interested Jean-Pierre. A former jazz player himself who had played with the legendary Louis Armstrong during a jam session in Lucerne, Jean-Pierre was delighted to actively endorse support for the London Jazz Festival in 2008. His bank would become the official sponsor of the event – the largest yearly jazz festival in the United Kingdom – as of 2013. Besides, Jean-Pierre was no stranger to the creation of the EFG Elements Series, a yearly selection of concerts for a large public audience, showing the extent and wide variety of the Festival's programme and modern jazz. EFG would also become a main partner of Estival Jazz Lugano, a free open-air concert festival organised in the centre of Ticino. In yet another display of Jean-Pierre's interest in jazz, EFG also invested in the musician Jeremy Monteiro, very famous in Asia, especially in Singapore. He would become one of the bank's ambassadors in 2008. New Orleans would award the title of honorary citizen to Jean-Pierre to thank him for his investment in the world of music.

Jeremy Monteiro [EFG]

Jean-Pierre Cuoni as a jazz player, 1960s [Demole Archives]

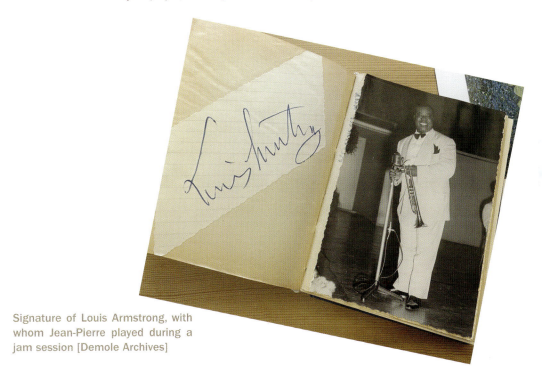

Signature of Louis Armstrong, with whom Jean-Pierre played during a jam session [Demole Archives]

An Active Retirement

*"If you don't know where you're going,
you'll never get there."*
Jean-Pierre Cuoni

In June 2014, Jean-Pierre Cuoni announced that he was going to retire. He wrote the following in March a year later:

> "As I announced last June, I will soon leave my position as Chairman of EFG International's Board of Directors. The members of the Board of Directors have suggested the election of Joachim H. Straehle as the new Chairman, subject to approval at the EFG International's yearly General Meeting on 24 April 2015. With his extensive experience in private banking, Joachim H. Straehle is perfectly qualified to contribute to the supervision of EFG International's future development as a leading independent private bank on the market. After a long and successful career with Credit Suisse, he has recently held the position of CEO of Bank Sarasin & Co. In the future, I'm happy to work with him as a member of the Board of Directors and as an ambassador of the company, which I will support actively."
>
> Jean-Pierre Cuoni

Jean Pierre Cuoni left his position as Chairman of EFG International's Board of Directors at the yearly General Meeting on 24 April 2015, at the celebration of the bank's 20th anniversary. Leaving only to come back stronger, should we say – after all, he remained a member of the Board while also staying on as an ambassador for EFG.

As he left the bank, its performance had been impacted by a series of external factors. This included market uncertainties, negative currency effects and persistent low interest rates, as well as the strong franc crisis brought about by the Swiss National Bank's abolition of the floor rate in January 2015.

The operating profit for 2015 was CHF 696.7 million, compared to 716.6 million a year before. Obviously, these were lacklustre profits. Yet they were still enormous, with an inflow of new capital at 2.4 billion and revenue-generating assets under management increasing by 3% at constant exchange rates, to CHF 83.3 billion. 2015 had above all else been marked by the formal deal concluded between EFG and the US Department of Justice regarding the bank's participation in the US tax programme as a Category 2 bank, with a negotiated one-off payment of 29.9 million US dollars.

In addition, there was a large-scale project brewing: the acquisition of the Ticino bank BSI! In July 2016, EFG's shareholders agreed to a capital increase to finance the acquisition of the Ticino-based institution, which would cost around CHF 1.33 billion[59]. The project would come about as EFG earnings were at a low due to a brief decrease of 8% in net profits from banking commissions and service delivery, a decrease in transaction-based revenue, low levels of client activity and the impacts of currency movements.

Of course, to face the many challenges that had been building up since 2015, the bank had embarked on a cost-cutting programme, in particular by closing its least profitable branches, which of course gave rise to critiques and controversy. In the end, however, the changes were clear. The consolidation with BSI paved the way for a transformation that would see EFG become the fifth largest Swiss private bank, with some 170 billion Swiss francs in total assets under management. As Jean-Pierre's successor said:

> "I am certain that the path we are taking is the right one, and that the potential for our future growth is definitely there."
>
> Joachim H. Straehle

These were high hopes as the world fell into what many observers felt was a real state of chaos. 2015 was marked by waves of violent attacks, especially in France. Meanwhile, the Middle East was overrun by the Islamic State, whose acts of terror would make the West tremble. 2016 was no calmer. Not only were there more attacks, but there were 327 other disasters, 191 of them natural while 136 were manmade.

President Obama, the First Lady and the Cuban President Castro observing a moment of silence for the victims of the Brussels terrorist attack, 22 March 2016 [U.S. Department of State]

The European Union would then watch in dismay as British voters decided on 23 June in favour of Brexit. In November of the same year, Donald Trump won the US presidential election, becoming the 45th president of the United States. This ushered in a new era of uncertainty. Obviously, Jean-Pierre Cuoni had chosen the right moment to retire. From a Citibank teller in 1957, in forty years he had built a banking empire, one that was respected and admired. He had invented the name "Private Banking", as well as a new form of contractual relationship with his company's employees, contributing to its success.

EFG in 2022

Five years after Jean-Pierre Cuoni's departure, EFG continues to move forward. In 2022, the bank ranks among the largest private banks in Switzerland, while developing its international business with some 40 branches around the world. The success of the CRO model invented by Jean-Pierre is undeniable. It still provides EFG's partners with originality and efficiency[60].

At the end of 2018, the bank's assets under management were up to 131.2 billion francs, outstripping analyst expectations – even if unstable markets and changing exchange rates caused an uproar for speculation. In February 2019, assets under management were up to CHF 146.4 billion, accounting for *Shaw and Partners*, an Australian group that EFG International just acquired a major share in. EFG's net profits in 2018 rose to CHF 70.3 million from a loss of 59.8 million in 2017. This is in spite of the acquisition of BSI by the Brazilian BTG Pactual in 2016, which, although almost doubling EFG in size, forced it to face huge challenges. BSI's implication in the Malaysian sovereign fund scandal 1MDB had led to the closure of BSI's branch in Singapore, as well as an order from the Swiss financial regulator demanding that it reimburse tens of millions of dollars in profits. This was an unprecedented sanction in recent Swiss financial history[61].

Still, these challenges did not slow EFG down. On 31 December 2020, the bank counted 3,073 employees and almost 159 billion in client assets, capitalising on average net new asset growth of 4 to 6% by 2022 as well as a revenue margin of at least 85 basis points and a return on tangible equity of more than 15%, the goal in mind being to return 50% of underlying profits to shareholders[62].

AN ACTIVE RETIREMENT

> "Since the Group's creation, an entrepreneurial spirit has shaped EFG and its employees. This spirit has given our relationships with our clients the necessary momentum to find the solutions you need quickly and easily. You can sum it up in a few words:
>
> We are a private bank with a business mindset."
>
> Giorgio Pradelli, CEO, EFG International

Chart, EFG Int. volume 2018 [marketscreener.com]

JEAN-PIERRE CUONI, A BANKER WITH HEART

Although he retired from business, Jean-Pierre still kept an eye on his bank's future. Although one of his favourite sayings was *"Es war kurz aber schön"* ["It was short but sweet"], he was still the founder of a multinational entity that he wanted to see flourish. As a result, he followed the bank from afar. Only his family was more important to him.

Private office of Jean-Pierre Cuoni [@ Noëlle Demole]

Jean-Pierre Cuoni's "five ladies"

After a long career, Jean-Pierre needed something to devote himself to for the next twenty years. He would choose his family: his wife Yvonne above all else, his partner in crime. Then of course came his daughter Caroline, who had become a mother herself.

Jean-Pierre and Yvonne [Demole Archives]

> "From today (the day of my retirement) my main occupation will be to take care of my 5 women."
>
> Jean-Pierre Cuoni

AN ACTIVE RETIREMENT

Caroline and her daughters Noëlle and Claire-Anne [Demole Archives]

Jean-Pierre had three granddaughters: Noëlle, born in 1992; Claire-Anne, born in 1995 and Marie, born in 2002. The banker became a real Papa Wolf, protecting his band of ladies from Day One. On a side note, Jean-Pierre and Yvonne hadn't hesitated to move to be right next to their daughter and her children. Sitting on his patio with a view on the lake, Jean-Pierre would read the newspaper every day while listening to classical music, opera or yodelling.

Jean-Pierre spoiled his family, taking them to Crete every year.

Jean-Pierre's band of ladies [Demole Archives]

"A life without children isn't a life worth living!"

Jean-Pierre Cuoni

Jean-Pierre and Noëlle Demole [Demole Archives]

Jean-Pierre and his granddaughters [Demole Archives]

Although he had always been a key part in the lives of the members of his family while he was overseeing the bank, after retirement Jean-Pierre became very present in the lives of his granddaughters. He would spend many happy days on the shores of Lake Geneva, filling out his collections and rushing to exhibitions, heading out to travel or to his

Jean-Pierre and his daughter Caroline [Demole Archives]

Jean-Pierre and Noëlle [Demole Archives]

second "home", Zermatt. A place to relax and reflect, Jean-Pierre spent a lot of time unwinding there with his loved ones, while also taking the chance to do his favourite activities: hiking and skiing. He had been skiing since he was a child, and he could never let a season of snow pass by.

Jean-Pierre and skiing throughout the ages: 1950, 1968, and the day before he passed away [Demole Archives]

According to Kafka, those who are happy never grow old; Jean-Pierre stayed eternally young. It's something that comes up again and again in accounts: he was a businessman and a banker, but also a faithful friend, a loving husband, an attentive father, a patriot who loved his country, an indulgent grandfather, a philanthropist and an optimistic dreamer with an everflowing supply of ideas:

Lonnie, Yvonne and Jean-Pierre [Demole Archives]

> "At age 79, I'm doing great because I'm happy, and I succeeded at life."
>
> Jean-Pierre Cuoni

Jean-Pierre and Yvonne [Demole Archives]

AN ACTIVE RETIREMENT

For everything else, he always shared his happiness with his family and his professional network. He had many chances to show off his cheeky sense of humour; once he would even wear a t-shirt with the inscription *"Sea, sex and sun"* during an important speech, just to cheer up the audience.

Every year, as per his daughter's wishes, Jean-Pierre made sure that he never missed Saint Nicholas Day. He had an important task: dressing up as Santa Claus along with a donkey, all for the amusement of his granddaughters.

[Demole Archives]

"Jean-Pierre was such a good man", many of his friends would say long after his death. What wouldn't he have done for his bank, his friends and his family? Especially as, at almost 80 years old, his building spirit was still intact!

[Demole Archives]

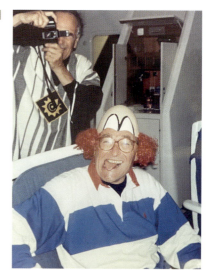

"God made a few perfect heads, the rest he covered with hair."

[Archives Demole]

Starting from little, an employee of an international bank, Jean-Pierre had climbed to the top through hard work and intelligence. Always modest, yet aware of the considerable means at his disposal, he put his resources to the service of others throughout his life. Jean-Pierre passed this spirit of generosity on to his eldest granddaughter Noëlle, giving her the same passion for philanthropy. Over 70 years old, he helped Noëlle come up with and establish an NGO that would function as easily and efficiently as many companies that Jean-Pierre had helped build.

Shere Khan Youth Protection

It was during a 2012 trip to the Silk City of Arni in the southern Indian state of Tamil Nadu that Noëlle would realise the gap between the rich and the poor. Moved by such levels of poverty, as an idealist she did all she could to help a six-year-old orphan she crossed paths with. Noëlle had been looking for a cause to devote herself to, and, as much as humanist as her grandfather, she knew how far her help could go. She quickly realised that she could develop a project, one she would refine with Jean-Pierre once she returned to Switzerland. It was in fact a very concrete idea, as it revolved around building an annex for the St. Mary's Jesus Home for children orphanage, which was suffering from an urgent lack of space.

Jean-Pierre had already supported the Right to Play international organisation for years, and was no doubt enchanted by his granddaughter's altruism. He didn't hesitate to help her when she told him about the unfortunate little boy she had helped, as well as her idea to build a new wing for the Indian orphanage. She also wanted to help young people by offering to finance their studies to get a job, the key to their futures. Jean-Pierre knew this concept well; after all, he had integrated the same principle in his bank. *"Make everyone a stakeholder", and that he had already supported the NGO SUEB beforehand by having financed a four-storey building, each of which bore the names of the banker's granddaughters and his wife. Grandfather and granddaughter embarked on a new project by developing an orphanage which would then be able to house 120 children and which would lead, in 2018, to the creation of the NGO Shere Khan Youth Protection. This would aim to get young people off the streets and allow them to start their studies.*

AN ACTIVE RETIREMENT

[Demole Archives]

JEAN-PIERRE CUONI, A BANKER WITH HEART

In a few years, Noëlle was able to spread awareness to a growing group of people and build a team on the ground to try to find a solution to the homelessness problem children faced coming out of the orphanage. This way, she hoped to guide the children so that

> "they will stay off the streets, where all the dangers are: trafficking, prostitution, etc. We don't want these kids to fall into that."
>
> Noëlle Demole

Shere Khan Youth Protection put almost 300 young Indians on the right track in 2021, much to Noëlle's satisfaction. Her grandfather would be particularly proud[63]!

Noëlle Demole, India, 2019 [Demole Archives]

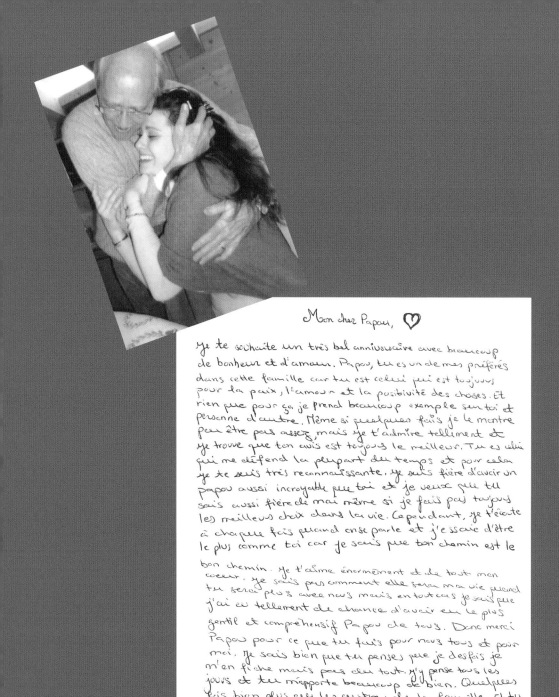

Mon cher Papou, ♡

Je te souhaite un très bel anniversaire avec beaucoup de bonheur et d'amour. Papou, tu es un de mes préférés dans cette famille car tu est celui qui est toujours pour la paix, l'amour et la positivité des choses. Et rien que pour ça je prend beaucoup exemple sur toi et personne d'autre. Même si quelques fois je le montre peut-être pas assez, mais je t'admire tellement et je trouve que ton avis est toujours le meilleur. Tu es celui qui me défend la plupart du temps et pour cela je te suis très reconnaissante. Je suis fière d'avoir un papou aussi incroyable que toi et je veux que tu sais aussi fière de moi même si je fais pas toujours les meilleurs choix dans la vie. Cependant, je t'écoute à chaque fois quand on se parle et j'essaie d'être le plus comme toi car je sais que ton chemin est le bon chemin. Je t'aime énormément et de tout mon cœur. Je sais pas comment elle sera ma vie quand tu seras plus avec nous mais en tout cas je sais que j'ai eu tellement de chance d'avoir eu le plus gentil et compréhensif Papou de tous. Donc merci Papou pour ce que tu fais pour nous tous et pour moi. Je sais bien que tu penses que des fois je m'en fiche mais pas du tout. J'y pense tous les jours et tu m'apporte beaucoup de bien. Quelques fois bien plus que les autres de la famille. Et tu le sais. S'il te plaît, fais moi confiance, je deviendrai quelqu'un de bien et je vais tout faire pour réussir dans ma vie comme toi. Et je serai toujours avec maman pour la soutenir même quand tu sera plus là. Tu peux compter sur moi.

Je t'aime,   Nos ♡

Epilogue

"Es war kurz aber schön."
Jean-Pierre Cuoni

After a lifetime of hard work, both in finance and in the home, and after a much-deserved retirement, the elderly man looked in on himself, reflecting on the path he had taken and all he had achieved. He humbly set his legacy in the hands of his descendants, as well as the belief that willpower and uprightness could move mountains, build empires and guarantee the future.

That morning on Saturday, 17 February 2017, the sun was shining on the Matterhorn, and Zermatt was waking up from a cold, peaceful night. It was a morning unlike any other. Jean-Pierre had passed away. The night before he had dined with his family, playing dead to scare his granddaughters and make them laugh. He had been thrilled a few moments earlier when a stranger had approached him to say he looked like George Clooney. Maybe he did it to shake off his own fears, seeing that his children were afraid of his passing? By dawn the next day, his heart had stopped. He had died with his eyes looking towards the sky and the light, as if his mind had fallen on yet another of those fleeting ideas that he had had throughout his life, the ones that had built his fortune. He passed away with quiet dignity in his wife's arms, a smile on his lips.

He left behind a great void in his wake. Those hours of sadness were also filled with calm, for though Jean-Pierre was gone, he was still with his loved ones. His spirit was still intensely felt in the hearts of his friends and family, his legacy still to be seen on the slopes that dominated the town, his adopted home. Yvonne often took care of him over the last few years, sometimes taking the risk of bothering him. She would tell him, "You must hate me sometimes given how much I annoy you!" He would tell her, "What are you talking about? I love you like crazy – and I have for 53 years!"

To hell with Keynesianism, Minsky's economic instabilities, the threats of systemic crises and the adaptive methods of stock regulation. Above all else, Jean-Pierre left behind him hopes and a reputation that had largely helped him make his bank, EFG, a success. As Adam Smith explained in his time, Jean-Pierre had been able not only to find a personal interest in his professional work, but also satisfaction for his clients and the protection of their wealth, helping them avoid the many pitfalls of the financial world. He was both generous and caring, qualities rarer than the most precious stones. Throughout his life he was a pillar of ethical behaviour, something he cultivated patiently and fervently. Not only did this bring him fortune and love, it also gave him a tangible aura of goodwill and confidence that all could see.

His ethics were all the more important given that the field he had helped develop, Private Banking, had known its issues. There had been inevitable scandals in many Swiss banking institutions, which had damaged the reputation of Swiss banks, even if at the beginning of the 21st century, Swiss banks managed roughly ten times the GDP of Switzerland and a third of all transnational private assets in the world. Everyone knows the rest: the end of banking secrecy, something some were afraid would happen!

Ethics, and an unshakeable moral code: that may be the real legacy Jean-Pierre offered to those close to him, pushing his granddaughters to achieve their goals while adhering to justice, truth and charity. The legacy of his work, beyond the personal characteristics of this exceptional man, is the one we wish to grant him. Who knows, perhaps one day his memory will become a hallmark, like Jean Monnet or Horace Finaly, who marked the first half of the 20th century as director of Banque de Paris et des Pays-Bas[64].

For now, let us close on these words from Prévert:

EPILOGUE

Le bonheur, en partant, m'a fait un clin d'œil,

Je sais qu'il reviendra, je ne porte pas son deuil,

Il ne fuit pas, il s'en va conquérant réparer d'autres écueils,

Pour me revenir encore plus grand, se reposer dans mes fauteuils.

Le bonheur, en partant, ne me quitte pas vraiment

Je sais que même de loin, il éveille mes sentiments,

Il entend mes hésitations et m'oriente résolument et surement,

Le bonheur est une étoile qui me guide par tous les temps.

Free translation:

While leaving, happiness winked at me,

I know it will come back, I will not mourn it,

It is not fleeing, it leaves in triumph to breach other hurdles,

Only to come back to me stronger, to rest on my chairs.

In leaving, happiness won't really leave me behind

I know that even from afar it awakens my feelings,

Hears my concerns and guides me boldly and reliably,

Happiness is a star that will always guide me."

«Un cœur bon et généreux s'est arrêté de battre»

Jean-Pierre Cuoni

8. août 1937 – 18. février 2017

nous a quittés brusquement au terme d'une magnifique semaine de vacances passée au milieu des siens.

Il était notre roc et n'a fait que nous couvrir d'amour.

Tu es désormais constamment à nos côtés

Yvonne Cuoni: son épouse
Caroline Demole: sa fille
Noëlle, Claire-Anne, Marie: ses petites-filles adorées

«Rien n'est plus beau ni plus simple à la fois qu'un amour humain partagé. C'est pour nous le signe le plus clair de l'amour de Dieu. Ce peut être aussi l'un des chemins les plus sûrs pour le rejoindre et participer déjà à sa plénitude».

Selon son désir, la cérémonie religieuse a eu lieu dans la plus stricte intimité familiale à Zermatt, où il repose désormais.
Cet avis tient lieu de faire-part.
En lieu et place de fleurs, un don peut être adressé à la Fondation pour laquelle il a œuvré pendant des années.
Fondation «Right to Play – Switzerland».

EPILOGUE

Annexes
a text by Jean-Pierre Cuoni

Probably one of my best decisions in my life I took in 1954, when I was 17. At the end of the first year of the Cantonal Commercial School I decided that I was tired of school altogether. I considered it a waste of time to continue towards a commercial diploma, two years out. For me it was clear, I wanted to work for an American Bank, because banking promised a great future to a young Swiss and since my greatest desire was to go to the USA eventually. I was keen in building an American base. The only American Bank in Lucerne then was the American Express Bank. My father was able to place me there as a trainee for a three year apprenticeship.

American Express Bank was a small Bank located on the thoroughfare of tourists, mainly Americans at that time, offering all cash-banking services to Americans, such as foreign currencies, check issuance and check payments, transfers, money orders, letters of credit, etc.,etc. in addition to securities and asset management services to local Swiss customers. We were only three staff and a boss, including 2 trainees. The boss did the asset management and the three of us did everything: from the execution of the customer generated cash transactions as well as stock exchange orders, keeping the books and customer ledgers, writing all the bank mail, reconciling correspondent bank accounts etc. etc., to brining the mail to the post office in the evening.

I really learned what banking is all about. My particular focus became the service at the counter as a teller (cassier). This is what I really liked and were I soon became a champion. Dealing all day long with clients and money meant: Be on your own, alone in front of the client, with a great deal of responsibility for your cashbox, working with precision and concentration, no right to make errors, at the same time achieve 100% client satisfaction under all circumstances and use many languages etc. At perhaps 18 or 19 of age, this was quite a challenge and when I compared this in my mind with what I would be doing instead at the school or what my former schoolmate were doing at the same time, I was convinced that I took the right decision to quite the school. These three years created the foundation of my future professional career and philosophy.

At twenty I entered the military service where I stayed for the better part of the following two years, with several intervals. During the intervals I was able to go back to Amexco to work as a teller. After two years (spring 1960) I became an officer of the Swiss army and was now ready to go on. My goal was the USA. Before that I wished to learn French "comme il faut". So, I decided to go to Paris I was told that Morgan Guaranty Trust was employing young Swiss. So I went there, got a job, but found myself surrounded by 20 other Swiss German. The purpose was to learn French and not to speak Swiss German all day long!! I learned through the news paper that First National City Bank of New York at the Champs Elysees was looking for a Teller. I applied and eventually got the job.. We were four tellers. The others were French, in their forties. The clients were mostly resident Americans and tourists. With my former Amexco experience it was easy for me to pull up a great show and to put my French colleagues behind. Within a few month, I was offered a three years Executive Trainee Program, at the end of which I was supposed to got to the New York head quarters. FNCB was planning at this point an important expansion in

Europe and to that effect they were hiring young Europeans as trainees to assure future European management .Clearly, I was thrilled and spent two years of intensive training. In 1963, the Bank decided to open a Branch in Geneva. Now, instead of going to New York, I was asked to go to Geneva, together with three senior Americans, to be part of the opening team. Disappointed on one hand, but exited on the other , I became the "bonne à tout faire" for my Americans and learned again enormously. The Bank opened at the end of 1963 and became fast very successful. Given this positive start, the Bank decided to open a branch also in Zurich and, how could it have been different, sent me in 1966 to Zurich to open yet another bank. In the meantime I also got married to Yvonne and in 1967 we had our daughter Caroline.

By early 1968 my mission of a branch opener was accomplished and I was now able to go to New York with my family. I was promoted to the position of a Credit Office in the European District at 399 Park Avenue. I was processing credit requests promoted by the European Branches through the Head Office credit approval mil!. Yet another new and valuable professional experience. I was also attending the NY Institute of Finance as well as bank internal training courses given by Harvard professors on Corporate Finance and Credit. All in all a very intensive and hard working period of time.

In 1970 I was called back to Switzerland, prematurely, as we decided to open yet another branch, this time in Lausanne. As the "resident branch opener", I had to go there. We took residence in Lausanne and I reached my first professional goal to became a Branch Manager. The party did not last very long. When in 1971 the USA quite the Bretton Woods Agreements the US Dollar started to float and indeed dropped from the 4.29 level maintained by the National Bank, first to below four but eventually as far down as to almost 1 to 1. Our business in Switzerland of lending Swiss France to US firms in Europe to finance their European expansion came to a immediate halt. All credits

Two of us, Bernard Dürr and myself had the answer. Lets do what the Geneva Private Banks are doing, namely take care of wealthy foreigners wishing to place their excess money in Switzerland. It seemed to us that FNCB, by now called Citibank, by definition had a lot of local clients throughout the world who had or were interested to have a "Savings Account" in Switzerland. It sufficed,, we said, to get introductions by the local managements and to call on these potential Swiss clients. We wrote a strategic paper, probably the first strategic paper ever written about soliciting potential Swiss clients, to solicit support for the idea from Head Office and from various focal management, particularly in the Middle East, where we identified the biggest potential. This was the hour of birth of Citibank's Private Banking, which has become over the forty-five years since then a major part of Citibank's activities. I soon became the Head of Private Banking for EMA in addition to CCO of Switzerland and by the time I left Citi in 1988, alter 16 years, we had produce some 15 billion of Client Assets. By the way, at the beginning we call it Citibank Private Bank, in line with other part of the Bank, Investment Bank, Retail Bank, Commercial Bank. But than we had a visit from Pierre Mirabeau, then Chairman of the Private Bankers Association in Geneva, telling us that this was not allowed. The title Private Bank, (Banquier Privé) was reserved for banks with partners with unlimited responsibilities. So, we simply turned Private Bank into Private Banking. Nobody intervened. But, the financial world was quick to embrace this new name for the activity of dealing with wealth management for private clients.

Jean-Pierre Cuoni

Our Story

In 1995 the seven founding members started a bank from scratch, based on an inventory of former private banking colleagues from Citi and Coutts around the world and on our "know how".

We introduced a new, unique business model and were driven by the conviction that we will succeed in view of the high quality of people we were able to recruit, and thanks to the equity participation executives and senior CROs were able to buy. At the beginning, we were all owners, not employees.

We found an ideal partner, who had embarked on a banking venture himself, and who welcomed our entrepreneurial model.

Together, we agreed to build a sizeable, global private bank and asset management business, with the goal to launch an IPO within ten years.

As of the beginning, our aim was to pursue rapid growth, organically and through acquisitions, and to become a "growth company". All executives we subsequently hired were entrepreneurs and dedicated to building a growth business.

The common target was an IPO in ten years.

After a couple of difficult start up years with little new business and P&L losses, most likely due to our brand (Banque de Dépôt), the situation turned in 1997 with the acquisition of RBS Switzerland, where we acquired a revenue base of CHF 6 Mio, eliminating most of their costs upon integration. This transaction put us on the map and triggered at the same time the change of name to EFG Bank.

In 1998 we broke even and in 1999 we produced a profit of CHF 5 Mie, enabling us to embark into Asia in 2000 with a CHF 7 Mio investment, i.e. we put at risk more than a full annual profit.

From thereon, rapid organic growth and a dozen of acquisitions took place, most importantly BEC, plus transactions from the Group, such as Monaco and the UK, enabling us to become eligible for an IPO by the fall of 2005.

At that time, we had CHF 54 Mio AUMs and CHF 120 Mio profits, the result of the hard work of 250 experienced CROs, located in more than 30 offices around the world. CGR over the preceding 5 years was above 50% per annum on AUMs and profits.

Indeed, the 250 CROs had produced on average CHF 40 Mio. AUMs per annum and per CRO. This extraordinary performance, unique in the market, was the result of our unique, entrepreneurial CRO model, which became eventually the IPO story.

On October 7th 2005 we launched a successful IPO, placing some 40 million new shares at CHF 38 per share, raising CHF 1.5 billion in cash and got listed with a Market Capitalization of CHF 5.5 Bio. The issue was seven times oversubscribed. Not bad, for a bank that got created only 10 years cartier from zero.

Investors bought our stock as a "Growth Stock" based on our past growth and positive future prospect thanks to our successful CRO model. We were expected to invest proceeds of the IPO into expansion of our CRO team and further acquisitions. At the IPO we promised to achieve CHF 300 Mio in profits by 2007 and CHF 100 Mio of AUMs. The stock was priced on this assumption.

Therefore, in 2005, two years before the worst financial crises since 1930, we were positioned and compelled to use our "war chest" of CHF 1.5 bio from the IPO to produce further growth through increasing the number of CROs and additional acquisitions.

Following the IPO we increased the number of CROs from 250 to over 725 by 2008, and made another dozen of acquisitions. We embarked on two new strategic directions, namely to invest in product related areas, such as Structure Products, Hedge Funds and Fund of Funds. At that time we felt that the internally generated fund business of over CHF 8 Bio justified such investment, and to expand into onshore markets, such as in the UK, Canada, Spain, Sweden, France and India.

By year end 2007, our record year, we had reached, CHF 107 Bio of AUMs and CHF 362 Mio of core profits, in line with our promise and market expectation created in 2005.

Our stock was traded at over CHF 60 per share in June of 2007, with a multiple of above 30 times current earnings. We had thus fulfilled all the promises we made at the time of the IPO. Initial investors were able to make a handsome profit on their investment.

It has to be recognized, that such unique and outstanding performance could not have been achieved without our aggressive drive for growth, exposing us to considerable future risks, at least on the short run.

Fatally, in early 2008 the sub-prime bubble burst, the financial market crisis got under way, and with the bankruptcy of Lehman Brothers in the fall, the hedge fund and fund of fund business fell apart, acerbated further by the Madoff fraud in December of saine year.

The party was over, the music had stopped. Volatile markets, distrust towards the financial industry and products and an extremely uncertain economic environment have been with us ever since.

Later, the Euro-debt crisis was slowing down further world economic growth, increasing the banking crisis once more. Clients lost confidence in financial markets and have become very conservative. They stay in cash. Banks have become the "bad guys", responsible for the general disaster, and distrust each other. A situation never experienced before, but still with us today.

At the same time the strengthening of the Swiss France against all other currencies made a considerable impact on our business. First, AUMs went down to some CHF 80 Bio by 2010, from CHF 110 Bio at the peak, without losing any client business, only based on currency moves. Second, with our Swiss hub function, we have almost 50% of our costs in Swiss Frances, whereas 95 % of revenues are generated in foreign currencies.

These two factors brought core profits down from CHF 360/2007 to 280/2008, 190/2009, 170/2010 million and to just a bit over 100 million in 2011. The revenue margin decreased from some 115 bps to 90, while the Cost/Income Ratio vent from 60 to 80%.

The deteriorating C/I ratio was particularly caused by our continuing to invest heavily in new CROs in 2008, when the crisis was already underway, on the assumption that the crises should not last for too long. With the ca 300 new

CRO hires in 2006/07 and 175 in 2008, we had some 475 CRO at the beginning of 2009 who had less than three years of experience with EFGI. Contrary to our previous experience, these 475 CROs had difficulties in building a business, as their former clients hesitated to move their accounts over to us during such uncertain times.

Also, perhaps more importantly, the quality of the new hires during these years had deteriorated considerably, as local executives often went for quantity rather than quality, in the aim to create growth at any price.

It took us indeed a very long time until we got the company to slow down on new hires. Needless to say, most of the hires of these years had to be eliminated later, creating nothing but useless costs.

In addition, the risks we were willing to accept in 2007 with our investments in product areas and onshore markets, turned post 2008 into casualties, one by one. While our core business stayed intact, based on loyal CROs and loyal clients, massive write offs had to be accepted, first on our product related investments and later on the onshore businesses. The total write off over 2010/11 will amount to around CHF 1 Bio.

Clearly, we would have needed more time, post investments, to foster each new unit and to integrate it better. The FF and HF businesses (and others) were run very independently by the sellers, often outside of our full control and influence.

In addition, most sellers, in general, had earn-out arrangements and were paid out annual profits subsequent to our take over, creating ever more goodwill on our books. When the going got tough, their own interest was very close to their hearts and disloyalties towards us were not uncommon.

The big question arises: "Were we wrong in making these investments into products and onshore activities"?

It can be argued that based on our former success, our own considerable position in HF by 2007, and the demand by wealthy individuals, offshore and onshore, for alternative products, the new strategic direction of diversification into HF & onshore activities was justifiable, while some of us had strongly argued against it. However, the timing was, of course, an absolute disaster.

Should we have known better? Perhaps! The question: "Why would so many entrepreneurs from whom we bought their businesses self at this particular moment in 2006/07?" can be asked. Did they have a better nose? Did they sense that this is the peak of the market?

What ever, during 2009 it became clear that we had arrived at a totally new economic environment and that there was no way back to "business as usual". The world had changed. Nothing was to be as before, particularly with respect to Swiss offshore private banking. Since future revenue creation became uncertain, strict cost control had to be implemented in 2009/2010. In hindsight, however, decided cost measure were not pursued and implemented aggressively enough, this most likely due to the deep-rooted growth culture prevailing at EFGI. While it was generally recognized by most of the managers that the organization was too big with to many underperforming sites, these same managers had difficulties in adjusting to the demand of reducing or eliminating staff or sites some of which were perhaps built just a very short time earlier.

Eventually, the continuation of the unsatisfactory performance in this dramatically changed business environment called for a change of leadership. In the middle of 2011, the board decided to appoint a new CEO, John Williamson, giving him the mandate to undertake a thorough business review and to adjust the organization to the new environment. John had redressed very successfully our UK organization and turned it into a highly profitable organization after a decade of suffering negative performances. He was thus the right man for the huge task ahead of us.

No question, Lonnie was the builder of our successful growth company. Thanks to his creativity, his energetic drive, his enthusiasm and determination for growth he was a great stimulator and motivator for all of us and together we have written this unique success story of Private Banking, second to none. We owe him an awful lot and shall not forget his accomplishments and thank him.

The subsequently announced new direction consists of our determination to go back to a pure private banking play, building on our proven CRO model with more emphasis on in-house asset management, disinvesting at the same time from product areas, including EFGFP, which will attempt an IPO, and reduce onshore activities, in addition to liquidating all unprofitable and/or mediocre businesses, companies, offices and CROs.

In the future, we will focus again on serving our loyal and high potential clientele by motivating and cultivating our reduced, but high quality CRO team (some 500 by now, ex FP), using increasingly our in-house asset management products.

We will make selective new hires of high quality only with proven track records, as we used to at the beginning. We will increase our business from existing clients as well as from new clients.

We will concentrate our business on the confirmed big centers in the four regions under dedicated regional management teams and further build our Asset Management capabilities. With other words: We go back to our roots.

But let's not forget, we have an impressive Core Business, of important size, made-up by thousands of clients of extraordinary quality and with future potential. We have a great team of professional CROs, looking after the CHF 80 billion of AUMs, guided by highly motivated managers and assisted by dedicated service staff around the world. This gives reason for very high optimism and we can all be proud of our past accomplishments.

Given impeccable deliveries on all fronts, we can get back to the CHF 100 Bio AUM mark, based on 5 to 10% p.a. growth, in a reasonable period of time. With a return of AUMs of 100 bps and a cost/income ration of below 75%, we can get back to a profit of above CHF 200 million in a couple of years.

The market will honor this by giving us a P/E of 12 to 15 times, (the days of P/ES of 20plus for banks are probably gone for long), and put thus our stock back at CHF 20.

Long term, however, given the new situation in Europe and particularly in Switzerland, I believe that we will need to partner with providers of

private banking services in Asia and Latin America, in order to penetrate better these obvious future growth markets and create a competitive edge for us.

The future for us is in these regions, where we have a strong position already under very strong local leadership and successful teams of CROs. Listing our stock in other exchanges than Switzerland is thereby not to be excluded.

LET'S GO FOR IT

Jean-Pierre Cuoni

Bibliography

Archives

Demole Archives

- Correspondence.
- Photographs.
- Miscellaneous.

State Archives, Lucerne

- AKT 413C773.
- "Cuoni".
- E. Cuoni & Cie 1909-1910 / A 1044/5673.

EFG International Documentation

- Announcement relating to Madoff, 19.12.2008.
- Press release, 16.03.2004.
- Yearly report 2005.
- Yearly report 2008.
- Yearly report 2011.
- Intermediate report, 31.10.2007.

Press

- Bilan
  - Fabrice Delaye, "Obama, notre meilleur ennemi" [Obama, Our Best Enemy], 2.11.2012.
- Journal de Genève
  - 30.03.1957/23.05.1969/29.08.1970/11.07.1972/12.12.1972/14.11.1972/6.11.1973/24.09.1974/6.05.1975/15.03.1978/16.09.1982/1.12.1982/17.10.1996.
- Financial Times
  - "Bank details revealed in Greek affair" 2.03.1990.
- Gazette de Lausanne
  - 11.11.1971/27.01.1984.
- Le Nouveau Quotidien
  - 2.04.1997/10.09.1997.
- Le Temps
  - Fabienne Bogadi, "Déjeuner avec: Jean-Pierre Cuoni, président d'EFG Private Bank" [A Lunch with Jean-Pierre Cuoni, Chairman of EFG Bank], Le Temps, 12.01.2004.
  - Sébastien Dubas "UBP rachète les activités de Coutts" [UBP buys Coutts activities], 27.03.2015.
  - Yves Grenier, "La chute de la BSI, le récit" [Recounting the Fall of BSI], Le Temps, 13.10.2016.
  - 27.07.2016/8.03.2008.
- The Independent
  - John Willcock, "Citibank sued over Polly Peck millions", 11.02.1993.
- The New York Times
  - Sonia Kolesnikov-Jessop, "Entrepreneurial Banker Uses Crisis to Consolidate", 1.05.2009.
- 20minutes
  - "Le patron of Novartis reste le mieux payé" [Novartis Boss Still the Highest Paid], 23.09.2008.

Interview

- Interview with Noelle Demole.
- Interview with Caroline Demole.
- Interview with Lawrence Howell.
- Interview with Thomas Muther.

Secondary Literature

- Sandrine Ansart, Virginie Monvoisin, "Le métier du banquier et le risque: la dénaturation des fonctions de financement du système bancaire" [The Banking Profession and Risk: The Denaturing of Financing Roles in the Banking System], *Cahiers d'économie Politique* 2012/1 (no 62).
- Swiss National Bank, *Les banques suisses en 1977* [Swiss Banks in 1977], 62, Orell Füssli Verlag, Zurich.
- Swiss National Bank, SNB Statistics department, *Les Banques suisses en 1995* [Swiss Banks in 1995], 80, Zurich, 1996.
- Swiss National Bank, *Quarterly report,* 1/2008.
- Dodis.ch/P5631 *"Pfyffer von Altishofen, Hans."*
- Hubert Bonin, *Histoire de la banque et des banquiers* [History of Banking and Bankers], Larousse, 1992.
- Gérard Bossuat (dir), *Jean Monnet, banquier, 1914-1945* [Jean Monnet, Banker, 1914-1945]. *Intérêts privés et intérêt général* [Private and General Interest], Comité pour l'histoire économique et financière de la France / IGPDE, 2014.
- Sophia Cantinotti and Jean-Henry Papilloud, *Histoire des banques en Valais* [History of Banking in Valais], Association valaisanne des banques (AVB), 2019.
- Erwin Cuoni, *Otto Zurmühle, Albert Benz: 150 Jahre Stadtmusik Luzern* [Otto Zurmühle, Albert Benz: 150 Years of the Lucerne City Orchestra], 1969, Lucerne.
- Luca Fasani, Francesco Lepori, *BSI fuori rotta* [BSI Off Course], Edizioni Casagrande, Bellinzone, 2016.
- Thibaud Giddey, *Histoire de la régulation des banques en Suisse (1914-1972)* [History of Bank Regulation in Switzerland (1914-1972)], Geneva, Droz, 2019.
- Sébastien Guex, *La politique monétaire et financière de la Confédération suisse, 1900-1920* [Monetary and Financial Policies of the Swiss Confederation, 1900-1920], Payot, 1993.
- Joëlle Kuntz, *Genève, une place financière. Histoire d'un défi (XIX-XXIème siècle),* [Geneva, a Financial Centre. History of a Challenge (19th - 21st centuries), Slatkine, Genève, 2019.
- Jean Morin, *Souvenirs d'un banquier français: 1875-1947*, [Memoirs of a French Banker: 1875-1947], Denoël, 1983.
- Becker William H, "Nixon, les échanges commerciaux et la fin du système de Bretton Wood" [Nixon, Trade Exchanges and the

End of the Bretton Woods System], in: Éric Bussière ed., *Georges Pompidou face à la mutation économique de l'Occident, 1969-1974* [Georges Pompidou against Economic Changes in the West, 1969-1974]. *Documents from the Colloquium of 15 and 16 November 2001 at the Economic and Social Council,* Paris, Presses Universitaires de France, "Politique d'aujourd'hui", 2003.

○ Raymond Zelker, *The Polly Peck Story: A Memoir*, Strathearn Enterprises, 2001.

Notes

1. Hubert Bonin, *Histoire de la banque et des banquiers* [History of Banking and Bankers], Larousse, 1992. See also: Sophia Cantinotti et Jean-Henry Papilloud, *Histoire des banques en Valais* [History of Banking in Valais], Association valaisanne des banques (AVB), 2019.
2. State Archives, Lucerne, AKT 413C773.
3. State Archives, Lucerne, "Cuoni".
4. State Archives, Lucerne, E. Cuoni & Cie 1909-1910 (Cote A 1044/5673).
5. Erwin Cuoni, *Otto Zurmühle, Albert Benz: 150 Jahre Stadtmusik Luzern* [Otto Zurmühle, Albert Benz: 150 Years of the Lucerne City Orchestra], 1969, Lucerne.
6. Dodis.ch/P5631
7. *Journal de Genève*, 30 March 1957, p. 2.
8. [https://www.gettyimages.ch/detail/nachrichtenfoto/er%C3%B6ffnungsrede-der-luftseilbahn-pilatus-luzern-1956-nachrichtenfoto/1174033926]
9. Interview with Noelle Demole.
10. Interview with Noelle Demole.
11. *Journal de Genève*, 23.05.1969, p. 5.
12. Membership in the AFBS was limited to members of the Swiss Association of Bankers, the umbrella organisation for Swiss banks. Swiss National Bank, *Les banques suisses en 1977* [Swiss Banks in 1977], 62, Orell Füssli Verlag, Zurich, p. 17. See also Thibaud Giddey, *Histoire de la régulation des banques en Suisse (1914-1972)* [History of Bank Regulation in Switzerland (1914-1972)], Geneva, Droz, 2019. http://dodis.ch/34597
13. Gazette de Lausanne, 11 November 1971, p. 13. The programme was under the responsibility of Vice-Chairman Gérard Mosseri Marlio, who oversaw its deployment from the Paris office.
14. Becker William H, "Nixon, les échanges commerciaux et la fin du système de Bretton Wood" [Nixon, Trade Exchanges and the end of the Bretton Woods system], in: Éric Bussière ed., *Georges Pompidou face à la mutation économique de l'Occident, 1969-1974* [Georges Pompidou against Economic Changes in the West,

1969-1974]. *Documents from the Colloquium of 15 and 16 November 2001 at the Economic and Social Council.* Paris cedex 14, Presses Universitaires de France, "Politique d'aujourd'hui", 2003, p. 133-153.

[15] *Journal de Genève*, 10 October 1970, p. 7.
[16] *Journal de Genève*, 29 August 1970, p. 5.
[17] *Journal de Genève*, 12 December 1972, p. 9.
[18] *Journal de Genève*, 11 July 1972, p. 7.
[19] *Journal de Genève*, 14 November 1972, p. 7.
[20] *Journal de Genève*, 6 November 1973.
[21] *Journal de Genève*, 24 September 1974.
[22] *Journal de Genève*, 6 May 1975.
[23] *Journal de Genève*, 15 March 1978, p. 15.
[24] *Journal de Genève*, 16 September 1982, p. 5.
[25] Fabienne Bogadi, "Déjeuner avec: Jean-Pierre Cuoni, président d'EFG Private Bank" [A Lunch with Jean-Pierre Cuoni, Chairman of EFG Private Bank], *Le Temps*, 12 janvier 2004.
[26] *Journal de Genève*, 1 December 1982, p. 7.
[27] *Gazette de Lausanne*, 27 January 1984, p. 15.
[28] "Bank details revealed in Greek affair", Financial Times, 2 March 1990.
[29] John Willcock, "Citibank sued over Polly Peck millions"; The Independent, 11 February 1993. See also Raymond Zelker, *The Polly Peck Story: A Memoir*, Strathearn Enterprises, 2001. This business scandal led to a reform of British corporate law, creating the UK Corporate Governance Code.
[30] Interview with Lawrence Howell, 2020.
[31] Sébastien Dubas "UBP rachète les activités de Coutts" [UBP buys Coutts activities], *Le Temps*, 27 March 2015.
[32] Fabienne Bogadi, "Déjeuner avec: Jean-Pierre Cuoni, président d'EFG Private Bank" [A Lunch with Jean-Pierre Cuoni, Chairman of EFG Private Bank], *Le Temps*, 12 janvier 2004.
[33] Interview with Lawrence Howell, 2020.
[34] *Les Banques suisses en 1995* [Swiss Banks in 1995], 80, SNB Statistics department, Zurich, 1996.
[35] Interview with Lawrence Howell, 2020.
[36] Interview with Thomas Muther.
[37] Interview with Thomas Muther.
[38] Interview with Noëlle Demole.
[39] Fabienne Bogadi, "Déjeuner avec : Jean-Pierre Cuoni, président d'EFG Private Bank" [A Lunch with Jean-Pierre Cuoni, Chairman of EFG Private Bank], *Le Temps*, 12 janvier 2004.
[40] Interview with Lawrence Howell, 2020.

41 *Journal de Genève*, 17 October 1996, p. 19.
42 Chaired by the historian Jean-François Bergier, the CIE published several intermediate monographs before delivering its final report in December 2001.
43 *Le Nouveau Quotidien*, 2 April 1997, p. 14. See also Fabienne Bogadi, "Déjeuner avec : Jean-Pierre Cuoni, président d'EFG Private Bank" [A Lunch with Jean-Pierre Cuoni, Chairman of EFG Private Bank], *Le Temps*, 12 January 2004.
44 *Le Nouveau Quotidien*, 10 September 1997, p. 12.
45 Yearly report 2005 – EFG International, p. 7.
46 Media release – EFG Private Bank, 16 March 2004.
47 EFG International – Yearly report 2005.
48 EFG International – Yearly report 2005, p. 10.
49 Sandrine Ansart, Virginie Monvoisin, "Le métier du banquier et le risque : la dénaturation des fonctions de financement du système bancaire" [The Banking Profession and Risk: The Denaturing of Financing Roles in the Banking System], *Cahiers d'économie Politique* 2012/1 (no 62), p. 7-35.
50 *Banque nationale suisse Quarterly report*, 1/2008.
51 EFG Report, 31 October 2007.
52 *Le Temps*, 8 March 2008.
53 EFG International, Release concerning Madoff, 19 December 2008.
54 EFG International – Yearly report 2008, p. 5.
55 Jean-Pierre Cuoni, EFG-International, Yearly Report 2011.
56 Fabrice Delaye, "Obama, notre meilleur ennemi » [Obama, Our Best Enemy], Bilan, 2 novembre 2012.
57 Interview with Caroline Cuoni, 2021.
58 Jean-Pierre Cuoni, EFG-International, Yearly report 2011.
59 *Le Temps*, 27 July 2016.
60 www.efginternational.com
61 Luca Fasani, Francesco Lepori, *BSI fuori rotta [BSI Off Course]*, Edizioni Casagrande, Bellinzone, 2016. Yves Grenier, "La chute de la BSI, le récit" [Recounting the Fall of BSI], *Le Temps*, 13 October 2016.
62 www.marketscreener.com/quote/stock/EFG-INTERNATIONAL-AG-163919/news/EFG-International-sets-new-targets-as-assets-rebound-from-2018-drop-28156027/
63 Interview with Noëlle Demole.
64 *Jean Monnet, banker, 1914-1945. Intérêts privés et intérêt général* [Private and General Interest], under the scientific direction of Gérard Bossuat, Comité pour l'histoire économique et financière de la France / IGPDE, 2014. See also Jean Morin, *Souvenirs d'un banquier français: 1875-1947* [Memoirs of a French Banker: 1875-1947], Denoël, 1983.